Tree and Bird, Stone and Star

The spirituality of witchcraft is experienced through the world around us, through nature, and through the bodies in which we live. The sense of the divine is not remote from the world, but is part of one's own being.

To be a witch means living in harmony with the ebb and flow of the seasonal tides and the cycles of sun, moon, and weather; to have a love of everything that lives, a respect for and sympathy with tree and bird, stone and star, and our fellow humans.

This is expressed through aligning oneself with the unfolding patterns of the ritual year, and the monthly waxing and waning of the moon. Witches believe that working in harmony with these cycles will nourish the spirit of the land while aligning their own spiritual development with the soul of nature.

About the Author

Elen Hawke is a British witch who lives in Oxford, England, with her husband and a house full of animals. She has one grown daughter and son. Elen is a photographer, illustrator, and has been a professional astrologer for twenty-seven years and a tarot reader for ten. These days, she divides her time between healing, teaching witchcraft, meditation, and chakra work, and celebrating the moons and festivals with the rest of the coven to which she belongs.

To Write to the Author

If you wish to contact the author or would like more information about this book, please write to the author in care of Llewellyn Worldwide and we will forward your request. Both the author and publisher appreciate hearing from you and learning of your enjoyment of this book and how it has helped you. Llewellyn Worldwide cannot guarantee that every letter written to the author can be answered, but all will be forwarded. Please write to:

Elen Hawke
⅝ Llewellyn Worldwide
P.O. Box 64383, Dept. 1-56718-444-8
St. Paul, MN 55164-0383, U.S.A.

Please enclose a self-addressed stamped envelope for reply,
or $1.00 to cover costs. If outside U.S.A., enclose
international postal reply coupon.

Many of Llewellyn's authors have websites with additional information and resources. For more information, please visit our website at http://www.llewellyn.com

IN THE CIRCLE

CRAFTING THE WITCHES' PATH

ELEN HAWKE

2001
Llewellyn Publications
St. Paul, Minnesota 55164-0383, U.S.A.

FIRST EDITION
First Printing, 2000

Book design and editing by Karin Simoneau
Cover design by William Merlin Cannon
Interior art by Carrie Westfall

Library of Congress Cataloging-in-Publication Data

Hawke, Elen, 1947–
    In the circle: crafting the witches' path / Elen Hawke.
      p. cm.
    ISBN 1-56718-444-8
    1. Witchcraft. I. Title.

    BF1566 .H377 2001
    133.4'3—dc21   00-062353

Llewellyn Publications
A Division of Llewellyn Worldwide, Ltd.
P.O. Box 64383, Dept. 1-56718-444-8
St. Paul, MN 55164-0383, U.S.A.
www.llewellyn.com

Printed on recycled paper in the United States of America

*For my daughter, my sisters, my mother, Stephen,
Kate, Mike, and Tereza; for Children of Artemis
and all my dear friends at witchcraft_uk;
for my brothers and sisters in the Craft; and for Louise,
who encouraged me to walk the path.*

Contents

VIII

....

C
O
N
T
E
N
T
S

Introduction

Years ago, when I began my first tentative search for information about witchcraft, I had a hundred questions to ask. There were many good books on the subject, of course, but not all of them had the answers I needed and a lot of them seemed to assume some prior knowledge on the part of the reader. So I began to find my own way bit by bit, piecing together the beginnings of a pattern that has grown broader and richer year by year.

I have been lucky. After a long period as a solitary, I did a series of workshops with a witch in London who gave me confidence and helped me find the inner empowerment I needed to honour my own truth and to believe that what I was doing was right. My path later led me through initiation into a formal Wiccan coven, then to the creative and fulfilling way I practice now, which includes teaching and solitary work. The warm friendship and mutually beneficial spiritual bond of the group of four to which I belong is very satisfying. I have learned so much from both my teachers and my students, and my spiritual life is rewarding in the extreme.

Since I started my search there has been an explosion of information on paganism—there are television programmes, hundreds of books to read, groups to join, and vast resources that can be explored on the Internet. Yet people are still seeking, much as I did, still wanting the same answers. My local occult bookshop directs potential students of witchcraft to me, and the guest books on pagan websites are full of the e-mail addresses of potential witches desperate for contacts and advice (I reply to as many as I can). The questions that come up again and again are: Where can I buy my magical tools? Do I have to make my athame myself? What should I put on my shrine? How do I learn about the elements? What do other people do and believe? How can I learn about ritual, spells, the eight festivals? Can I be a real witch if I wasn't born into a family of hereditary witches? These are just a sampling of the many questions that are asked.

This book is for all those seekers who stand where I once stood. I hope it will give inspiration and knowledge to those who read it, and the confidence to reach for inner truth; for to become a witch is to answer a call of the heart, and that call will be heard differently by each of us. Because of this, the material I have written is a collection of guidelines and suggestions, interspersed with how *I* have experienced the flow and rhythm of the year's cycle, how *I* have interacted with the powers of the ritual circle and Goddess and God. Although these experiences are personal to me, I hope that they will stand as examples of how ritual material can be formed and shaped and lived. But they remain only guidelines. Each of us will know these things differently and every perspective will be valid, yet there will be common ground, just as there is shared communion within sacred space.

Above all, I want to reassure those who are looking for the right way to be witches that we are all our own best teachers. Although we share a set of basic tools within the

Craft, we will all use them differently and no two people will share the same understanding. Each must choose their own road; the most anyone can do for somebody else is to act as a signpost pointing the way.

THE WHEEL OF THE YEAR
CLOCKWISE STARTING AT TOP CENTER: OESTARA (MARCH 21),
BELTANE (APRIL 30 TO MAY 1), SUMMER SOLSTICE (JUNE 21), LAMMAS (AUGUST 1),
AUTUMN EQUINOX (SEPTEMBER 21), SAMHAIN (OCTOBER 31 TO NOVEMBER 1),
WINTER SOLSTICE (DECEMBER 21), IMBOLC (FEBRUARY 1)

CHAPTER ONE

Winter Solstice

December arrives with a growing sense of hope as we move toward the Solstice. In my garden, redstarts (thrush-like birds) greedily strip the berries from the holly. A few tattered leaves cling to the apple trees, and the remains of the fruit lies rotting at the base of the trunks. Mornings are crisp and cold, the dawn sky clear above the slumbering oak. The frogs have abandoned the pond and are wintering elsewhere . . . mostly in the woodpile, as we can tell by the sound of the sleepy croaking when we fetch in logs for the fire. Some days are blustery and brisk, with gulls wheeling among shredded gray clouds. But mostly there is a profound feeling of peace, which seems to be born of the rising earth energies so clearly felt on days when the trees are rimed with frost and the ground is hard.

At this time of year when I walk by the river, or sometimes in my garden, I see a single wren, the tiny bird that was sacred to the druids and belongs to the Holly King, the God of the waning half of the year whose rule is from Summer to Winter Solstices. His counterpart, the Oak King, whose bird is the robin, reemerges as Sun King at the Winter Solstice, thus symbolising the sun's return to power. These two were once believed to fight for the favour of the Goddess, each giving way to the other in turn to rule over a six-month period. So the cycle of death, regeneration, and rebirth, so often denied in our modern society, is clearly seen in the rise and fall of the year's rhythm, the turning of the seasons, and the nurturing of new life that will emerge from its formative sleep when winter's barren coldness ends.

We celebrate the Solstice with friends; a warm family-like gathering where food is shared, children are welcome, and both Yule fire and candles are lit before we exchange presents.

Later, when the sky is dark and stars burn bright in the cold air outside, our small group of four meets within the circle upstairs in the bedroom that serves as a temple for sabbats and moon rites. In the northern quarter, the altar is adorned with holly, ivy, and mistletoe as well as our magical tools and altar candles. In the circle's centre, a large black cast-iron cauldron contains an unlit candle, greenish-white like the mistletoe berries. The altar candles and point candles are lit, and in their glow we stand to quietly breath, letting go of all the excitement and hassle of the day, breathing calmly . . . breathing out stress . . . breathing in tranquillity . . . chakras opening, good energy rising, till I sense everyone is ready. Moira consecrates the water, blesses the salt, and then sprinkles the mixture around the circle's edge, asperging each of us, cleansing, purifying, beginning the step-by-step process of building sacred space, removing us from the everyday world.

A spicy smoke drifts across the room as Robin sprinkles incense on charcoal and carries the censer round. Moira laughs and my *husband Nick coughs as Robin smudges all of us thoroughly then returns the censer to the altar.*

Now I take up my athame, raise it to the northern quarter in salute, and begin to cast the circle, sending golden-white energy out through the blade, drawing a barrier of protection around us that will keep away stray thoughts and dull the sounds reaching us from the world beyond this room. I begin to speak as I reach the eastern corner of the room, "I call up Thy power, O circle . . . be Thou a boundary of protection . . . " till I have come back to the north again and we are sealed into magical space, a place set apart from our everyday lives.

We have already decided to call in a quarter each. Robin begins with the east and air and we tease him gently because it's his favourite element even though he is an earth sign by birth. His summoning is powerful and we all feel the breeze that momentarily stirs the yellow eastern candle. Then Nick brings in fire and the south, Moira water and west, and I stand ready to call in the northern quarter of earth. This element is the strongest at Yule, and as I stand here now I can feel the weight and depth of the winter soil so strongly that I expect to find it piling against the wall of the room. I see standing stones, I see the stars wheeling in the black midnight sky above high mountains, I see bare branches. The still-ness is so immense that I am lost in its depths, rooted into my inner reaches, till I speak the words of invocation and I am back in the warmth and companionship of the circle, though the peace remains.

At this point we would usually raise energy and then call in the Goddess and God, but this time the pattern of the ritual itself will bring them in.

We put out all candles to signify the darkness from which the sun is reborn . . . giggles as Robin fumbles for the matches, which we will need again later . . . then quiet for a moment except for a bit of shuffling around. Then begins a slow, steady drumbeat, like the pulse of a great heart, and woven into that Robin's voice, though deeper and quieter than usual:

Under stone, under bone,
Into the earth, await rebirth,
Into the tomb, into the womb,
In darkness hold, still and cold.

There is absolute silence as we all, in our minds, in medita-
tion, go down, deep down into earth, stone, the cave-womb from
which the tender infant light will come forth.

Unbidden, images flood my mind: the sun burns red through a
thin mist; the season swells with the promise of birth and rebirth
as again the Wheel comes round; root and sap prepare, in their
cold sleep, to surge into life at the appointed time; and again and
again. And he waits, curled in fallen leaf, wrapped in bark and
moss and loam, ready for that still point of darkness before it all
begins once more. Whatever we have done, whatever the damage
and pain, renewal will manage its act of healing. Love suffuses
me and I reach for my bodhran, my Celtic drum, begin to beat
out a light, exultant rhythm, the signal for the kindling of the
cauldron candle—the point of light in the womb of the Goddess.

Faster and faster I drum till the insistent beat gives way to
Moira's voice as she cries, "The child of promise comes to us out
of the tomb, out of the womb!" We each light our personal candle
from the central flame then look at each other in wonder, washed
with waves of joyous power, then link hands and spin that energy
faster, sending it out to carry healing and peace into the world.
Nick has relit the point candles; we are blessing the food and
drink and relaxing together, enjoying the enchanted aura that sur-
rounds us, gradually coming back to a more prosaic state of mind
before we open the circle again.

Many religions, including Christianity and Mithraism, echo
the theme of the Child of Promise. Jesus was born in a stable
and Mithras in a cave, both surrounded by animals. Stable

and cave represent the earth womb, the womb of the Goddess from which the light . . . the son . . . returns. In ancient times, when people believed that only the power of their rituals could bring back the sun, celebrations did not fall on the Solstice but three to four days later, when the days could really be seen to be increasing in length.

The Winter Solstice, or Yule, which falls between December 20 and 22 (this varies from year to year) as the sun enters Capricorn, is a solar festival. It is sacred to the Oak King, and to the reborn Sun Child of whom Mithras, the Celtic Mabon, and Jesus are representatives. Traditionally, it should be celebrated at midnight.

Now the light will begin to wax again, imperceptibly at first, as the sun is reborn and the days start to lengthen. The Oak King challenges and triumphs over the Holly King, as light and warmth will eventually vanquish dark and cold. Yet we need the inward turning and rest that winter brings, need the descent into inner contemplation to nourish our psyches.

In ancient times, the returning light was celebrated a few days after the Solstice because then people could see the days were lengthening. This is why we now celebrate Christmas Day on December 25 and not December 21. When Christianity came to Britain it usurped the pagan festival dates, and so the birth of Jesus was assigned to the date of rebirth of the Celtic Sun God.

The wheel of the year seems to stop and time hangs suspended as the longest night heralds the return of the light. Even though the Goddess now is the White Goddess of frost and snow (death and cold for those of us who live in northern lands), she becomes the mother as she gives birth to the Sun God. Now is a time of joy and hope when creative forces begin to rise again, though they won't become obvious till Imbolc, the festival of purification in February when the first hint of spring appears.

The God as Sun God and antlered stag is reflected in the old carol "The Holly and the Ivy" in the line "The rising of the sun and the running of the deer . . . "

The house and altar are decked with holly for the Holly King, ivy for the Goddess, and mistletoe for fertility; its white berries like sperm and its green leaves overlaid with a golden solar glow. Mistletoe grows more commonly on apple trees: to the Celts the apple was the fruit of death, and mistletoe stood for fertility and birth; but the most sacred mistletoe was that which grew on the oak, the tree of the waxing year and the cycle of growth, the king of the forest to the druid priesthood. The wren and the robin are traditional, represented in the current age on Christmas cards. At one time the wren was hunted and killed at this time of year to represent the death of the Holly King. Before the days of central heating, people's lives were harsh and the death of the old cycle was eagerly welcomed as a preparation for the return of light and warmth as the sun waxed in power once more.

We kindle our Yule fire from an oak log, always saving a piece from last year to set fire to the new log, thus continuing the neverending cycle. A sunwheel (a cross within a circle, representing the solar festivals of two solstices and two equinoxes) can be made from branches and decorated with holly, ivy, and ribbons. Foods at this festival include those flavoured with cloves and spices, which once would have disguised the rancid taste of long-stored winter foodstuffs.

In our personal lives, this is the time to take stock of where we stand and what we want before moving toward spring. The life forces are stirring but need time to gain strength before fully emerging.

So begins another turn of the year's wheel, the seasonal cycle of moons and the eight solar festivals.

CHAPTER TWO

Goddess and God

Witchcraft is both incredibly old and very new. It undoubtedly has its roots in the remote past, drawing influences from our Neolithic ancestors and their stone circles, the mighty Egyptian temples, Greek initiatory rites, the Celtic seers, and the herb and hedgerow lore of the medieval village healer. However, it owes much of its current form to more recent influences as well, and many of the patterns of practice are borrowed from the early twentieth-century occult societies, Hindu systems of chakras and karma, and the beautiful and inventive input of modern witches themselves.

The spirituality of witchcraft is experienced through the world around us, through nature, and through the bodies in which we live, and all these things are regarded as sacred.

The sense of the divine is not remote from the world but is part of one's own being. To be a witch is to be in touch with life on the truest of levels. It means living the essence of life in harmony with the ebb and flow of the seasonal tides and the cycles of sun, moon, and weather; to have a love of everything that lives, a respect for and sympathy with tree and bird, stone and star, as well as our fellow humans. At the core of the Craft is a quest for personal growth along with a desire to protect and sustain the world we live in. These two aims are expressed and experienced through aligning oneself with the unfolding pattern of the ritual year, and the monthly waxing and waning of the moon. Witches believe that working in harmony with these cycles will serve the dual purpose of nourishing the spirit of the land whilst aligning their own spiritual development with the soul of nature. This awareness of the rhythms of the natural world is even present in busy cities, where many witches now live and practice.

Many people associate witches primarily with the moon, but they are equally of the earth. There are different ways to be a witch, from closely following nature, using plants as remedies, and sowing and reaping at the right phases of the moon and planets, to practising formally in a way that verges on ritual magic. Witchcraft ranges from simple herb lore to deep philosophy and a study of the stars. It can be earthy, basic, and spontaneous, or carefully planned and dramatic; it can be solitary and meditative, or ecstatically, dancingly shared.

A high proportion of witchcraft channels its sense of the ineffable through a duality of deity, the Goddess and the God who are seen as universal and yet also as part of the natural world, of the cycle of growth, decay, and regeneration. To some witches, Goddess and God are metaphors; to others they are beings in human guise who can be appealed to, much as one might take a request or complaint to a higher but approachable authority; and still to others, they are transcendent super powers who can be sensed within the confines of ritual space. But whatever the personal interpretation put on them by individual witches, to many in the Craft there is not one focus of devotion but two. Some traditions put more emphasis on the importance of one or the other of this pair, but a duality it remains, and the whole of the ritual year revolves around this.

The Wheel of the Year, of the seasons, moons, and eight festivals, is complex because we have inherited more than one cycle from our ancestors, a rich blend of the traditions of the hunter-gatherer peoples and of their later agricultural successors. The many energies interplay: one summer may be wet, a winter mild or harsh, spring late or early; and the festivals may fall on any point of the moon's round. The yearly cycle never repeats itself exactly.

The hunter-gatherer cycle is simple. The Oak King wins the favour of the Goddess and thus rules from Winter to Summer Solstices. During his time, the days lengthen and grow warmer, nature flourishes, and everything is productive. Then, at Midsummer, he is challenged by the Holly King, who defeats and slays him. Thus we are brought to the waning half of the year when the forces of growth begin to withdraw, the sun loses its power, and darkness and cold are in the ascendant.

The later, the agricultural cycle, is far more complex and reflects the round of sowing, cultivating, and harvesting of crops and the raising of livestock. The God is born from the Goddess's womb at Yule and she returns to her maiden state with the purification of Imbolc. At Oestara—the Spring Equinox—Goddess and God range wild and free to mate at

Beltane and marry at Midsummer. At Lammas the Goddess is the harvest mother who surrenders the fruit of her body, which is represented by the God who dies as the corn is cut down. The Goddess is pregnant with the new Sun King, yet her energies begin to return into the soil and the long approach to winter commences. Life is always present in death, and death in life. At the Autumn Equinox she receives the fallen seeds that are ready for spring germination; she will nurture the seeds during the winter months as she mourns the passing of the God from the world, even though he gestates in her womb awaiting rebirth. Then, at Samhain, the God stands at the gates of death, the passage between the worlds, allowing those in the world of form and those discarnate to be reunited briefly in love. So the Wheel turns round to Yule once more and the God is reborn.

This is the yearly pattern that (albeit embellished in recent times) has grown out of northern European and Celtic traditions, and it matches the climate and seasonal inceptions of this region, though it has been adopted by pagans from other parts of the world. However, other traditions are sometimes practised alongside or woven into it. In particular, the legend of Demeter and Persephone is popular, with the Maiden Persephone bringing light and growth from Spring to Autumn, and her mother Demeter plunging the world into winter in mourning for her daughter's return into the underworld. But even within regional legends, which are attuned to earlier or later summers and winters, a sense of duality is still apparent.

With regard to this sense of duality, one should beware of becoming too entrenched in Jungian concepts of masculine and feminine (animus and anima). Both sexes manifest qualities of compassion and nurturing as well as aggression, extroversion, and competitiveness. Some pagan groups assign strict gender roles to their members while others are more flexible, allowing women to call in the so-called masculine elements and men the feminine, and encouraging the traditional roles of priest and priestess to be adopted by anyone. Other groups are single gender and so both roles have to be taken on by one sex, and may consequently be assigned to only one of the two deities. It is all a matter of choice and the important thing is to maintain a balance whilst working in a way suited to your own temperament and needs. Within my group, the whole process is democratic and we take it in turns to assume various roles and tasks within ritual. This does not make us better or more correct, it's just the way we happen to do things and it suits us. I myself have been part of a strict Wiccan coven and have found a beauty and rhythm to the rigid assumption of male and female roles as well.

The Goddess

Her pregnant womb is the ground of being from which everything arises. She is the swelling bud on the branch, the life that bursts forth in response to the fertilising sap of the God. She is egg and nest, raindrop, curving breast, the swell of the landscape. She is the earth that gentles the dormant seeds awake.

Hers is the force that drives the storm; the quiet dissolution that brings decay before new growth can come. She is the heartbeat of the universe.

She is present in the smallest thing yet embraces dimensions beyond the mind's comprehension—yet we, too, contain them and embrace them. There is nothing that is not inside her or does not include her. We are Goddess, all of us. We are not separate from or different to her or each other. All of life contains all life. Without her we could not live, but without each smallest particle of being she would have no existence. The interdependence of life is absolute, yet each part is unique.

The Goddess to me is my beautiful teenage daughter brushing her long blonde hair, or spraying on perfume before meeting her boyfriend; she is the women around me coping with their children, living their lives to the full; she is the memory of my strong, determined grandmother who trained as a teacher at the turn of the last century, cut her hair against her husband's will, and won a bronze medal in the Olympics. The Goddess is also myself, fighting and winning the battle to birth my child in my own home . . . she is women everywhere who fight for the rights of themselves or their families. She is the universal sisterhood that binds me in mutual understanding to my female cats and dog as well as to my women friends, my mother, my sisters, my daughter. She is the intuitive force in men too.

She is death and new beginnings, destruction and growth. She is the spiral of growth that shows equally in a snail's shell, in DNA, and in our own spiritual paths.

Over countless ages the universal force we know as Goddess has taken on many faces and many forms according to the climate, temperament, and understanding of the people who have believed in her. In Neolithic times she was the bird goddess; to the ancient Egyptians she was known as Isis, Hathor, Nepthys, Nuit, Maat, and many other names; to the Greeks she was Artemis, Demeter, Hecate; to the Celts Cerridwen, Arrianrhod, and Brighid. She lives on in Christianity as Mary the Virgin whose forerunner was Isis, and the bird goddess of so long ago is still with us, albeit masculinised, as the Holy Spirit.

Many animals are sacred to the Goddess, among them the cat, the hare, the dove, the bee, the cow, the pig, the snake, and the horse. She is symbolised by circles, spirals, eggs, shells, holed stones, the cauldron, the chalice, and round and fecund shapes. Apples and figs are her special fruits, and among her plants are the ivy and the rose.

To modern pagans, the Goddess shows three faces. At the new moon she is the young Maiden: independent, fierce, and carefree. Hers is the time of fresh beginnings when creative ideas are rising within us. Rituals at this time are centred around the initiation of new projects. At the full moon she becomes the Mother, pregnant with that which is soon to be brought to fruition. Magic worked at the full moon is very powerful—the cosmic tides are at the flood and psychic senses are enhanced—and rituals are centred on bringing fully formed ideas into manifestation, whether we are asking for healing or for something else that we need in our lives. Then at the end of the cycle, when the moon is a slender waning crescent or is dark, she becomes the Crone or Hag, filled with wisdom as she nears her own rebirth once more as the Maiden. This is the time to let go of all that holds us back, to dissolve blocks, to banish that which is harming us or is no longer needed. Inward reflection and introspective self-analysis also bring their rewards now because the energies at this phase are so still and calm.

The cycle of menstruation and fertility in females of many species is linked to this pattern of waxing, fullness, and waning (as are other matters pertaining to inception, growth, and fruition). For many women, menstruation occurs at the new moon, thus beginning a new fertile phase (by the time the blood flow starts, the fresh cycle has already begun); ovulation occurs on or around the full moon, the time of maximum fruitfulness; and the premenstrual phase coincides with the waning or dark moon when the old is shed to make way for the new.

Many threads have been woven into our current Goddess tradition, but the pattern we are making is entirely our own as we pull all the elements together into something our modern minds can relate to and use. Thus, old goddess forms take on new meanings, and Greek and Egyptian goddesses rub shoulders with Celtic and Sumerian, sometimes even within the same ritual space!

> We cannot love only the light,
> The stars burn in the night sky,
> And I, woman,
> Shelter the womb's dark mystery
> At the spiral's end.
>
> In the centre, united perfectly,
> No this or that,
> Only the nestling one into one in stillness—
> In stillness the dance of life contained
> to flow into being again.

The following gives a brief description of some of the best loved goddesses. More information can be gained from reading the many excellent modern books on witchcraft, Wicca, and paganism.

Isis

She was the Mother Goddess of Ancient Egypt, sister and wife to Osiris, who was the Egyptian version of the vegetation god. When Osiris was dismembered and his body parts scattered, Isis searched far and wide to put him back together, later bearing a child by him (a variation on the theme of the Goddess who sees her lover sacrificed with the corn and then bears him again at the commencement of the new solar year—borne out by the role of Isis as goddess of grain and harvest, and her relationship with the underworld where she goes to search for her husband). Her veneration spread throughout the ancient world, even arriving in Britain with the Romans. Occult groups at the turn of the last century placed great importance on her, as do many present-day pagans. To many people she is the Queen of Heaven and also the Queen of Nature, roles similar to the Priestess and the Empress in tarot. Because she became merged with Hathor, the cow goddess, in later Egyptian dynasties she is often shown with horns on her head that frame a disk representing the sun or the moon. Frequently, she is seen with wings extending from her outstretched arms. She was preceded by the Sumerian Inanna and has been succeeded by Mary who has taken over her symbols of dove, rose, blue garments, and suckling child. To witches she represents compassion, peace, maternal love, strength and fortitude, and the living soul of nature.

Sekhmet

Another Egyptian deity, Sekhmet has the body of a woman and the head of a lioness. She is a solar goddess as is shown by the sun disk on her head. Hers are powers of destruction and creativity, of anabolic and catabolic resonance. When you want to clear some obstacle from your path and turn the released power to creative use, then call on Sekhmet (or the force within all of us all that she represents). She is feminine courage and independence and fierce protectiveness. Her wisdom is the wisdom of the heart. Her colours are fiery golds and oranges, amber, and bronze.

Brighid

Another solar goddess is the Celtic Brighid. She is a triple goddess and her three selves represent healing, poetry, and smith or metal craft. She originated in Ireland but has associations with local goddesses throughout Britain. She is represented by eternal fire, by tools of metal working, and by forces of regeneration and creation. Her special time is Imbolc and she is connected with the bodhran. There was once a shrine to her in which a fire was tended by priestesses so that it never burned out. When Brighid became Christianised as Saint Brigit, the shrine became incorporated into a convent where nuns kept the flames alive for many centuries. Draw on her influence when you need inspiration with anything creative or help with healing, particularly with emotional or mental conditions.

Elen

A long time ago I had a series of visions arising out of meditation. In them I was in a forest somewhere and a woman was there, sometimes standing under the trees, sometimes bending over me, and sometimes running along a well-trodden path. She was young, clothed in a long green dress, and had hair the russet red of autumn beech leaves. Sometimes I saw her with antlers on her head, sometimes not, but usually she had leaves caught in her hair or clinging to her clothing. There was a sense of freedom about her, a hint of wooded uplands and wild open spaces. I mentioned the vision to a friend; she told me I was seeing Elen, goddess of the ancient trackways, who is at times connected with the paths the reindeer make on their migratory journeys. Although I am attracted to this deity, I have never felt compelled to call upon her during ritual; I think perhaps she is coming into people's consciousness at this time because we need to wake up to the environmental crisis facing us all. Meditating on her brings a deeper and deeper connection with untamed nature, wild animals, and the beauty we will lose forever if we don't do something about the rapid erosion of our rural spaces.

Cerridwen

Cerridwen was originally a Welsh goddess and has deep associations with the Crone aspect of the Goddess and the underworld—as shown by her connection with the pig, an animal of the Goddess that has chthonic associations. She owns a magical cauldron that has the power to transform or bring wisdom to those who partake of the liquid brewed within it, just as we may gain wisdom by bringing up and transmuting subconscious material.

Oestara

The Christian festival of Easter is named after this Saxon goddess, as is estrogen, the female fertility hormone. Her time is the Spring Equinox, when nature is replenished or reborn, symbolised by eggs, lambs, chicks. Her sacred animal, the hare, has become the Easter Bunny. In fact, hot-cross buns, often associated with Jesus and the crucifix, derive from the cross within a circle, which is the sunwheel of the solstices and equinoxes.

Freya

Like Oestara, the Nordic goddess Freya, wife of Odin, has links with the spring and fertility. She is another goddess of nature and the earth, like Isis. She is also a goddess of love, in the same vein as Aphrodite or Venus. Amber is associated with her through the magical necklace Brisingamen. The cat and the swallow are animals that belong to her. Her flower is the daisy.

Hecate

Hecate is the Crone goddess of ancient Greece. She is a lunar goddess whose time is the dark phase of the moon. She is also connected with crossroads and the underworld, both places of transformation where one way may be relinquished or abandoned and another taken up, thus bringing change and forward motion. If we fear change, then Hecate will seem grim and implacable, for when called on she is uncompromisingly thorough in her severing of the things we have outgrown or outworn; but if we let go willingly she will be a loyal friend and guide, lovingly showing us the way to healing and new development.

Demeter

Demeter is also a goddess from ancient Greece, a deity of fertility and growth who rules over the full moon. She is most often linked with the grain and with livestock. It was she who plunged the world into winter when Hades abducted her daughter, Persephone, and carried her off into the underworld. Her bargain with Hades for the release of Persephone for half the year was believed to have defined the seasons. Thousands of people over hundreds of years were once initiated during her seasonal rites at Eleusis. Her particular animal is the pig, the creature associated with the Goddess all over the world and across many religions.

Artemis/Diana

Artemis is huntress goddess of Ancient Greece, sister to Apollo. Diana is her Roman counterpart. Both are virgin goddesses and yet are deeply involved with midwifery and childbirth. Artemis is the Lady of the Beasts, Maiden of the New Moon, she who is seen with a deer by her side and arrow and bow across her shoulder. Diana has become the

Goddess most revered by many feminist or lesbian witches, and an all female branch of the Craft, Dianic Witchcraft, is centred around her.

There are many other goddesses from different cultures, but similar themes link them; earth or Mother goddesses have characteristics in common as do Maiden or Crone goddesses. Furthermore, the definitions pass over from one phase to another, so deities of the Mother phase may have underworld connections in common with the Crone, who in turn may give a hint of the regenerative qualities of the Maiden. The Goddess is one, even though she shows three faces and many identities.

The God

He is active growth energy, rising sap, the greening of spring, the dying power of autumn, the richness of the living forest. He is both healer and taker of life. The god force provides the impetus for growth and change in nature, which we trace in the solar cycle and eight festivals, following his birth, youth, mating, fathering, and dying.

He is the lord of the dance of the universe; he is fire in the blood; he is creativity, male sexuality, fertility, eroticism, and earthy enchantment. He can be puckish and mischievous, but he also represents all that is best in men: protectiveness, compassion, and nurturing; the strength to cry openly and to admit to vulnerability and fear; the ability to express anger without violence. See the pride and protectiveness in the eyes of a new father holding his baby, and you are seeing the God. He is father, brother, lover, friend, protector, comforter.

He is both son and lover to the Goddess, a concept perhaps alien to modern society and yet which holds a deep symbolism—for the force that fertilises her is also that which grows and fruits within her. We see it again in human society, for women all over the world mother their men even while revelling in their physical strength.

There are several aspects through which we know the God and they are different but not mutually exclusive. He manifests as the Oak and Holly Kings, but also as the dying and resurrecting vegetation or corn god who flourishes then dies with the crops. He is the many sun gods known to ancient times. He is Shiva, Osiris, Bel (the sun god from whom we take the name of Beltane), Apollo, Cernunnos, Herne, and Pan, to mention only a handful of the names and identities people have given him. We know him as the Horned One, the antlered stag, and the Green Man, whose face in stone adorns churches and cathedrals.

His animals include the stag, the bull, the hawk, the goat, and the ram. His symbols are phallic shapes such as the wand or tall standing stones. His plants include the holly, the oak, mistletoe, thistles, and sunflowers.

There is a tendency in modern paganism to play down the God and concentrate on the Goddess, and this is understandable in the light of our contemporary struggle to emerge from patriarchy. However, Goddess and God are intertwined, are dual aspects of a whole, and to emphasise one at the expense of the other is to create the sort of destructive imbalance that has caused such misery in global society during the thousands of years of male dominated religions.

As with the Goddess, modern witchcraft enjoys an eclectic mix when it comes to the god forms brought into ritual, and this reflects the extent to which many cultures have influenced each other throughout history and the willingness of pagans to take what they need during their spiritual search.

Lord of the Greenwood, eyes a-flashing,
Sparks flaming, horns glancing.
Leaves dancing, dancing, dancing,
Dancing my blood awake.

Yield to the rhythm of the heart's drumbeat,
The tide of the year,
Of madness, gladness;
Spiralling, turning, dancing, dancing,
Dancing my soul awake.

The forms the God takes can be grouped under two main types: solar gods and horned gods of the earth or otherworld.

The Antlered God

The hunter god of northern Europe has regional identities as Cerne, Herne, and Cernunnos. Many places are named after him, such as Herne Bay in Kent and the Cerne Abbas Giant in Dorset. He wears the antlers of his animal, the stag, and these represent his beast self, his connection to nature, and sexual energy brought to the spiritual centre at the crown of the head. He is the ancient fertility god of the Greenwood who, along with other horned deities, was demonised by the early Christian missionaries, being given the persona of the Devil in an attempt to turn people away from his worship. He is the Lord of the Animals who watches over all creatures, but particularly the wild herds. He gives and heals life, but he takes life, too, culling the irreparably wounded and sick; for this reason he is feared as well as loved—though he brings death only when it is unavoidable and clears the way for the new to be born. At Samhain he becomes the Lord of the Underworld, opening the gates of the Otherworld so that the living can greet their ancestors and those they have recently lost. He is fertile, rampant, sexual, fierce, and passionate, yet he is gentle, tender, protective, and kind. The Celts pictured him with a torque (an open-ended circlet of plaited metal) round his neck and snakes twisted round his arms.

Pan

Pan is a god from northern Greece. He has the horns and lower body of a goat, showing his sexual nature. Sometimes he is shown playing a set of reed pipes. Pan is more mischievous and playful than Cernunnos, causing panic and excess, tempting us to go a step too far, yet bringing us laughter and merriment. He started life as a minor deity but has enjoyed elevated status in recent times. To many pagans he is interchangeable with his antlered northern European counterpart.

The Green Man

You can see his face carved in stone in cathedrals and churches all over Europe. He can also be found on pub signs and cut into the brickwork of Victorian municipal buildings. He has origins in the eastern hemisphere as well. The Green Man is sometimes shown as a man's face with leaves bursting forth from his mouth and curling into hair and eyebrows, sometimes as an almost human face constructed entirely of leaves. He is a symbol of the vegetation cycle, the greening of nature in the spring, the flourishing of plants and their eventual sundering or dying back in autumn. He is often shown made entirely of oak leaves, a clue to his connection with the stag god, Lord of the Forest, and, of course, the Oak King. He is universally popular among pagans of all persuasions and is probably the sign most associated with paganism by the general public.

Lugh

Lugh, whose name means radiance or light, is a solar deity who was widely worshipped during the Celtic period. Lammas, the festival of first harvest, was also named Lughnasahd after him. He is the master of all skills, the bringer of light out of darkness. Lugh originated in Ireland, but may have associations with the Welsh Llew, husband of Blodeuwed the flower maiden, as well.

The Mabon

He is the Celtic Child of Promise, the divine child of light born at the Winter Solstice. In legend, he is said to have been stolen away soon after birth and imprisoned in the Underworld, later to be rescued and released, surely symbolising the liberation of the sun's light after winter darkness. He has musical skills and is depicted playing a harp. The Celts are said to have accepted the substitution of Christ because of similarities between the two deities.

Witches seem to focus on fewer gods than they do goddesses, and most people I know concentrate their attention on the Horned God. However, classical, Celtic Norse, and Mediterranean sources yield many more examples of gods whose qualities may be drawn upon during ritual.

CHAPTER THREE

Imbolc

The days are growing longer. The snow of January has melted, giving way to heavy but intermittent rain. In the small stone ring at the end of the garden, snowdrops are blooming, and the spears of crocuses are pushing through the brown debris of autumn. Although it is still cold, I sense that spring is drawing closer, and though we wake to bitter mornings when the pond is crackled over with a thin layer of ice, plants and animals are beginning to awaken. There is a dainty sprinkling of yellow where celandine stars the lawn beneath the lilac tree, and buds are forming on apple and rowan. The black starkness of the hawthorn is softened by swelling points of green.

At dusk we all arrive at Sally's house bearing milk, cakes, cheese, snowdrops, candles, and twigs of early catkins and pussy willow. In times gone by every village would wait in darkness for a maiden of the community to rekindle their fires as she went from house to house with her rush taper, till the symbolic light of spring had been brought back to every home. Now Mandy, Sophie, and Gemma, our own small maidens, come in from the kitchen solemnly bearing their burning white candles, giggling a little as they push slipping crowns of greenery back onto their heads. We praise them and light our wish candles from the ones in their hands and push them into the earth-filled cauldron. We are welcoming Brighid, whose festival this is.

Later, alone, I sit in the quietness of the circle. It is dark as yet, but a cauldron of water with snowdrops and floating candles has been placed in the centre of the room and there is a single white candle on the altar in a small earthenware bowl of compost.

I meditate for a while on the winter darkness that will soon recede, thinking of all I want to cleanse from my life at this festival of purification. There is recent illness to eliminate, there are worries that are fading but still need to be expunged, and there are the one or two failed or abandoned projects I want to leave behind.

When I am ready, I lean forward, put a match to my white Goddess candle on the altar, and cry, "From the depths of the winter soil, the Cailleach's dark fastness, the light now returns."

I ponder for some minutes on the symbolism of the waxing light, born at the Solstice and now gaining strength, thinking about how, as nature is beginning to manifest signs of growth after the long winter sleep, so in my own life the deep inward spiritual contemplation from Samhain to now is starting to ease into more outward pursuits as I anticipate the creativity of spring and summer. Everything seems so fresh and full of possibilities at this time of year and I am eager to ditch anything that isn't working and try something new. It seems somehow easier to let go right now.

Saying, "As the light grows, so the first signs of spring emerge," I kindle the floating candles with a taper lit from the

Goddess candle. They are icy white with little bits of glitter embedded in the wax and look incredibly pretty drifting around on the surface of the water among the snowdrops. The room is filled with a quiet happiness. I become aware of the presence of a woman with plaited red hair, a circlet of gold around her forehead. She is not as I would have imagined Brighid (in fact, my rational mind shies away from personifying the Goddess), but she is undeniably here in the room with me, so real she is almost visible to my physical eyes. Later I will want to explain it to myself, but for now I accept the experience without question.

Words pour from me unbidden, seemingly bypassing my mind and flowing straight from my heart: "O, Lady Brighid, this is your festival of fire and water. May I be washed clean of all I wish to leave behind me as the earth is washed clean by the rains ready to germinate new growth under the waxing fire of the sun. I let go of all that has outlived its purpose in my life, that the fresh and new might flourish."

As I speak, the room seems to fade back, giving way to a track that winds between young birches. Beyond the striped gleam of their trunks, the track crests a small rise and bends out of sight. On either side, the ground falls away into mist, but the path is firm and there is light ahead. Intuitively, I know the vision is telling me that my half-formed ideas and wishes will lead me to something rewarding that I am, as yet, unable to see. The birches represent birth (in this case a new direction), and the mist is the uncertainty out of which the solid way forward arises.

The images fade and the room grows real again. I whisper, "Lady, may your love and strength nurture my new direction as you nurture the spring seeds."

When the circle is open, I put the Goddess candle on my shrine to burn out overnight. For growth spells involving the planting of seeds, I will use the earth during waxing moon rites.

Imbolc (pronounced *Immolc*) is a cross-quarter fire festival that lasts from January 31 to February 2 and falls in Aquarius. It is sacred to Brighid, the Irish goddess of poetry, healing, and smithcraft. Imbolc should be celebrated in the early evening when the sun has recently set.

Although many groups call in the God as well, to me this is almost entirely a Goddess festival, the only one of the eight in which the God is alluded to but not present.

In ancient times this festival was called Oimelc, which means ewe's milk, as it was the traditional time for lambing. Because of this, Imbolc is a fertility festival linked with conception. This is further emphasised by the germination of seeds and the first glimpses of spring. The connection with lactation means that dairy foods are traditionally eaten now.

Imbolc is a time of deep cleansing and purification. The February rains wash the soil clean of the dross of winter, making them ready for spring sowing; and so we can also be cleansed of the old in preparation for new growth in our lives. This is a time of rebirth after the dark days of winter, and the light reborn at the Solstice now emerges and grows.

Symbolically, the Goddess is purified after the birth of the God at Yule. She is restored to virginity in the old sense of becoming her own person again. Candlemass, which falls on February 2, is the Christian version in which the Virgin Mary is purified following the birth of Jesus.

There is a second theme at this festival, that of the Corn Bride. At Lammas the Corn Mother went into the burial mounds and entered her Hag phase, becoming the Cailleagh in keeping with the darkness and cruelty of winter. Now she comes forth as the Corn Bride. Originally, the Corn Bride was made of corn or wheat at Lammas. She was dressed in white at Imbolc, then taken from house to house by the women of the community. On the first day of February she was laid in a rush basket, her marriage bed, with an acorn tipped wand by her side to represent the God's phallus. She was attended by the women until the lights in the community had been doused and rekindled by the chosen maiden to represent the return of light after winter. After this the men were allowed to join in the ensuing feasting.

Snowdrops and white candles are used at Imbolc to represent purification. A white candle can also be burned as a wish candle to represent a seed to be germinated in one's life that will grow through the waxing half of the year.

Building a Shrine

A shrine is a special place that contains personal objects that represent the way you experience and express your spirituality. Although other people can offer you guidance and suggestions, what they choose is a reflection of their own preferences, so ultimately it is better to make up your own mind. Let your intuition guide you; have fun with it and you will be fine.

Building up a personal shrine is also a very good way to learn about the elements, the seasons, and the Goddess and God. It can be a spot in which you keep your magical tools when they are not in use, or you may decide to put those somewhere else and keep your shrine for other objects. It can be cluttered or minimalist, adorned with ornate statues and pictures, or simple and natural with a few shells and pieces of driftwood. You may even decide to try a different theme from time to time. But however you initially plan your shrine, it is almost certain to grow and evolve with you.

Any shelf, chest, or covered box can become a shrine, even a space on a dressing table. I have found that small shrines have grown around my house over the years. I will put a new Goddess figure somewhere and she will immediately begin to accumulate crystals and stones and flowers around her . . . it's quite unplanned . . . it all seems to happen organically.

Get a feel for where the best place for your shrine will be. Of course, you may be limited by your environment, but try to put it in a place that feels right. There seems to be a point of optimum balance for each article in a room (and for each object on a shrine) and things will be more harmonious if this point can be found. They can be moved into other harmonious relationships later, of course. You may find that the direction in which your shrine is placed dictates what you put on it over a period of time, even though you may not be fully aware this is happening. My shrine is on a low oak shelf in the west of the room. I suddenly realised one day that a lot of things on it related to water and the west. I have a statue of Isis that I painted faience blue (a deep green-blue), plus shells, two dark blue bowls, and a miniature cauldron. There is a mirror above it, too. I have other things on the shrine that don't relate to water, such as my ritual equipment, a spiral ammonite fossil, and other Goddess statues, but even so, the predominant feel is of water. Nick's shrine is in the east and has feathers, *three* incense burners, and a box containing jars of incense. Furthermore, my shrine is in a corner that never gets full daylight while Nick's receives the eastern light at dawn. It has all evolved without conscious motivation on our parts.

You can also build a shrine in the garden, maybe under a favourite tree or by a pond. A shelf can be built with stone slabs, candles, and maybe a God or Goddess placed on or under it. If you prefer, you could use a log instead. Garden shrines have a wonderful feel and are good places to get in touch with the natural world and the seasons. As you sit there, you can hear birds singing and almost feel things growing. The trees may speak to you after a while, and small creatures will forget to be afraid of you if you are still enough, and may come closer. If you don't have a garden, use a balcony or window ledge, or a place by an open window in summer.

In front of your shrine is a good place to sit in meditation—providing, of course, that there is room. It can become a focus for study where you put symbols of a phase you are entering or some aspect of witchcraft you are working on—a tarot card or Goddess image would be examples of this. You might want to add flowers, fruit, corn, or other seasonal gifts to help you relate to the eight festivals. Candle or cord spells can be left on the shrine while they are in progress. You may pick up an interesting stone or feather when on a walk and later feel it has qualities that remind you of the Goddess or God or one of the elements. Anything is apt because it is your space and you make the rules.

Some people have one shrine, while some have different shrines for the different elements; for instance, they would have feathers, incense, their athame, and yellow or blue things in the east; candles, their wand, and red things in the south; shells, a cauldron or chalice, water bowls, and blue things in the west; salt, a bowl of earth, a pentacle, and green or brown things in the north. I have worked with people who had this arrangement and also brought out a central altar when they performed rituals: they used to take the magical tools off the separate shrines and put them on the altar during the rite.

You will probably want to include something to represent the Goddess and the God. These can be natural things like a bunch of oak leaves, deer antlers, or a ram's skull for the God, and a small cauldron, a stone with a hole through it, or a conch shell for the Goddess, the latter being representations of female genitalia or fertility. Alternatively, you may want to acquire statues or carvings of the deities. If you do the latter, many new age or occult shops and online stores will have examples. You can sometimes find appropriate figures in museum shops. My Isis came from a shop in London, near the British Museum, which imports the statues from Egypt. We have two Horned God figures, one bought in Bath and one in Glastonbury. I have a beautiful little Inanna figurine carved out of shed deer antler. It is possible to find tasteful figures if you are prepared to look around. Don't be tempted to grab the nearest thing for the sake of having a Goddess or God on your shrine. The right things will come to you if you are patient and determined—or you can do magic to draw the images you need.

Go for statues or objects that attract you, ones that speak to you. A lot of people like the classical Greek and Roman deities. Personally, I prefer the Neolithic, Egyptian, and Celtic images . . . we are all different in our tastes, our spiritual responses, and in the past life influences that have contributed to our makeup (if you don't like the idea of reincarnation, substitute historical/geographical bias for the last statement). Tuning into these figures or articles is a way of learning what Goddess and God mean to you personally. Just having those things in your environment will start to awaken an intuitive response from you that can be developed and enhanced by lighting a candle on your shrine and sitting in meditation or quiet contemplation. Be receptive; don't be repressive or judgmental about the intimations that come to you—Goddess and God are speaking from their place in your inner heartspace where you know rather than reason. These objects aren't Goddess and God, but they are symbols that point to a reality we can't encompass with our everyday minds, and concentrating on them will lead you to subconscious revelations that will gradually come to the surface of your awareness in a way that has meaning for you.

Of course, there is no law of witchcraft that says you have to have a shrine; it's perfectly acceptable not to have one if that's what you prefer. Not everybody relates to spiritual iconography. After all, these are only interpretations of something we can't grasp and that we therefore personify to try to make it more real to ourselves. What would the Goddess look like to a rat or a snail or a being from another galaxy? Is she separate from ourselves? Does she even exist other than as a vehicle for our understanding of life? Do what you feel is right for you and don't let anyone tell you that you are wrong. The idea is to create a sense of the sacred experienced as part of the daily fabric of your existence. To achieve this you must act from the heart. How we perceive and express our spirituality is a deeply personal thing, and rightly so, for though we are linked to each other and the rest of life, we are all unique.

CHAPTER FIVE

New Moon

Outside, the birds are still singing, but quietly, as dusk washes the spring sky with shades of green and lilac in which the planet Venus glows like a solitary lamp. The moon's indigo disk lies cupped in its own silver rim.

In our room shadows are pooling, springing into energetic life as we set a match to each of the point candles. Earlier, I picked three white daffodil buds from the mossy ground under the apple trees, and now they gleam on the altar, radiating freshness.

Nick and I stand for a while, centring ourselves, opening our awareness to the dynamism of the moon's current phase, tuning in to each other, till we are ready to cast the circle. When we come to raise power I drum a light and rapid beat that seems to quicken without my intent. The eastern candle flares briefly as

Nick utters the invocation that will welcome the goddess: "Maiden of the new moon, be with us now. Bring your bright enthusiasm and freshness into our lives. Hail and welcome!"

And there she is, dressed in white, flowers in her hair (seen in our minds' eye and sensed all around us). The pulse of the circle quickens. Puffs of sharp-sweet incense flurry and disperse. I feel a strange pressure on my brow. Later, Nick tells me that he had glanced at me just then and caught a glimpse of a silver crescent curving up to meet my hairline.

Now we call on her horned mate who brings green fire into our space so we feel encircled by rising sap and budding leaves. The air around us throbs, dances, exquisitely electric. We are laughing, grinning, wanting to abandon ourselves to that dizzy intoxication. But dancing is for outside rituals . . . the old floorboards of our bedroom won't take too much stress, so we content ourselves with calmer movements.

We seat ourselves near the altar and each take a small handful of sunflower seeds from the central pentacle, cupping them in our hands, picking them up one at a time to infuse them with the strength of our wishes. These seeds represent new projects or aspirations, that which is coming into being and needs time to form and grow. Nick wants to find a new career path and to develop the confidence to follow it, the courage to seize the right opportunities. I have similar needs regarding my creativity. We are careful not to overload the ritual with too many wants, not because that would be greedy, but because it is difficult to pour the same determination into several goals . . . and it is determination that nourishes spell work.

Nick reaches for the bowl of earth we have prepared and we plant the seeds one by one, voicing our intentions, reducing each affirmation to simple key words: "Success," "Creativity," "Courage," and so on till all is voiced and the seeds are pushed into the moist brown loam. Then Nick points his hazel wand at *the bowl, channelling the electrical charge around us, directing it down into the bowl of seeds. I can sense and almost see the silvery ribbon of energy as it ripples from the tip of the wand into the bowl.*

When Nick has finished I pick up the bowl, feeling a tingling in my fingers as I do so. "Lady of the new moon, Lord of the Spring-time Forests," I say, "as the moon waxes, may these seed ideas take root and flourish, becoming manifest in the world of form. So mote it be."

"Blessed Be," we both intone.

This bowl will be left on Nick's shrine till the seeds sprout and can be transferred to pots and later the garden. We trust that the ideas they stand for will become similarly visible and will flourish, taking the form that is right for us, growing gradually but healthily. Past experience has taught us that our magic will bear fruit, though we cannot yet guess how and when the results will manifest.

The work is done and it remains only to bless and share our chalice of spring water and plate of buttery crescent moon cakes before opening the circle to the world again.

At the new moon, sun and moon occupy exactly the same degree of the same astrological sign so that if, for instance, the sun is in Aries, the new moon will be in Aries, too. The moon is dark and will not become visible for two to three days. For magical and spiritual purposes it is best to wait till the first slender crescent appears in the sky before doing work involving increase, though the tempo starts to rise from the inception of the moon into its new phase. A good time in which to let new ideas become more tangible prior to developing them is before the moon becomes visible. Later, when the moon can be seen as a curve that grows daily, the pulse of her energy quickens, activity becomes more outward and worldly, and ideas become less abstract and begin to take root. The world around us seems filled with activity and we can get a lot done each day.

For new and waxing moon rituals, put budding or opening flowers on the altar, preferably in pale colours or white. The type of incense used now should be light and sharp or flowery; damiana or lemon grass would be good examples. A pure white candle lit when the crescent is first seen will radiate a lovely bright essence when it is lit on successive evenings. From now till first quarter is the time of the Maiden, and rituals are concerned with fresh ideas, new beginnings, and anything that needs to progress from embryonic form. From new moon to first quarter the Goddess moves from birth to early childhood and then puberty.

CHAPTER SIX

Oestara

In the early mornings frost drifts like snow in the shady hollows of the woods, where early bluebells thrust up through the jigsaw of fallen brown leaves. The days are warm when the sun comes out, but brisk, chilly breezes drive white clouds across the sky and set the daffodils dancing. In the hedges, blackthorn bushes are decked with sprigs of creamy blossom and glossy new greenery, and on the roadside banks primroses flower. Birds are singing, building nests, laying eggs. The whole of nature seems to be thrusting and mating and burgeoning and generally behaving in a thoroughly abandoned manner! The pond is full of frog spawn, toads are emerging from the pile of old leaves at the bottom of the garden, and at night we hear hedgehogs snuffling and grunting (our cats are confused by them; when they try to catch

the hedgehogs they roll up and present a formidable ball of prick-
les). Spring has undeniably arrived.

On the morning of the Equinox, Moira and I drive out to the
Rollright Stones and walk around the main circle. Someone has
obviously performed a ritual here already and a sunwheel lies
between two of the small, pitted standing stones. The rest of the
circle seems to be coming alive, getting ready to dance, a current
of energy running between the stones and their guardian pine
trees. I look out across the fields to the low hills beyond and it
seems as if a heat haze blurs the view, though it is cold enough for
us to be glad of our coats.

We leave and walk along the road, cutting down the side of the
field that leads to the Whispering Knights, once a burial mound
but now a group of stones that lean together without the support
of soil to hold them up. On the path that leads to the stones we
feel as though the earth is alive, vibrating with power. Moira says
she feels this was a processional way. I feel it too, sense that at
one time youths and maidens came this way to pay homage to the
ancestors before performing their spring rites. The thought crosses
my mind that perhaps I am being fanciful. Simultaneously, a hare
starts up from almost under our feet and races away across the
plough land. I smile . . . this is the Goddess's own animal . . .
was it coincidence that it appeared just then?

When the stones are reached, I lean my back against the railings that protect them and unzip my drum from its case. There is
nobody around to be disturbed by the sound, so I let the stick roll
across the skin, raising an answering pulse from the earth, a
throbbing beat that is felt by the body rather than heard. They
are not my ancestors whose spirit lives on in this place—thousands of years separate their age from mine—but still the heartbeat of my drum connects us and the power of the earth comes
spiralling up, matching the twisty shapes of the Whispering
Knights themselves.

At dusk, when the four of us are together in the flower-filled "temple" with its masses of yellow, green, and pink seasonal candles, my drum gives back the earth's pulse, filling the room with the essence of the stones, the echo of a time, and a world beyond our imagining. With reverence we light a white candle from the black one on the altar, thus symbolising the balance at this time between dark and light, with the light about to increase. What we ask for now is balance and harmony in our lives and between ourselves and the land. We can't go back to ancient times . . . and anyway, they had their problems, too (Robin points out that the destruction of the environment began in Neolithic times). But we can learn to live on this earth with more harmony and sensitivity.

Oestara, or the Spring Equinox, is a solar festival that occurs on or around March 21, the first day of Aries, and marks the coming of spring. It is sacred to the Saxon Goddess Oestara. At this time, day and night are of equal length all over the world. In Celtic times this was a state that was neither one thing nor another, neither day nor night being greater, and, therefore, was magical. This festival should be celebrated at either dawn or dusk, which are also in between times, poised as they are between day and night.

Light and dark are in balance, but the light will soon become ascendant, so this is a time of resurrection and rebirth (Christianised as the resurrection of Christ). Because of this, eggs, a symbol of rebirth whose golden yolks represent the sun, are decorated and eaten. We keep some of ours till the following year then dig them into the garden prior to decorating new ones, thus keeping the theme of death and rebirth alive year after year. Sunwheels can be made from pliable thin branches like willow, then decorated with daffodils or forsythia. Many people eat hot cross buns; these are mini sunwheels, with their solar cross in the centre representing the two solstices and two equinoxes.

Everything in nature is stirring now, beginning to flower and mate. The hare, sacred to the Goddess, dances in the fields. His present-day representation is the Easter Bunny, another symbol of fertility. The Goddess is the Spring Maiden from whose footprints flowers grow as she passes; the God is maturing into manhood; their passionate courtship is the fire that drives the fecund abandonment around us. We, too, are preparing for outward growth and expansion in our lives, eagerly pressing forward with confident new plans.

The flowers at celebrations should be predominantly yellow for the early spring sun: daffodils, narcissi, primroses, forsythia, and winter jasmine. Burn pastel candles: pale yellows, blues, greens, pinks, and mauves. Seeds can be blessed and planted to represent new projects.

CHAPTER SEVEN

Magical Equipment

Strictly speaking, we don't need magical tools during ritual, as circles are cast and magic is performed by the power of the mind. But tools help us to focus our energy; they bring a sense of specialness to what we do; gradually, they become imbued with our own power and with the purpose for which they are used, so that just picking them up helps us to shift into the right mood and level of consciousness for the work we are about to perform. Tools we make ourselves become impregnated with evocative vibrations very quickly because we concentrate on them intensively while we craft them, but equipment acquired from others can eventually feel just as much "ours," and there are ways of speeding this process up. One method often recommended is to sleep with the article under one's pillow. I'm sure this works perfectly adequately, but I have never fancied trying to lie with my head on a knife or a wand or a deck of tarot cards (I know someone who bent her cards permanently out of shape by doing this!). I find that just handling the object regularly does the trick . . . especially in the early post-acquisition days when you want to admire and possess. I sometimes rub ritual tools with a favourite essential oil like bergamot or geranium. The best way of all to forge a bond with the implement is to dedicate it in ritual and then use it for the purpose for which it was designed: if it's a drum, then play it; if it's an athame, use it to cast a circle. At the end of this chapter I will provide a simple ritual to dedicate an athame. This can be adapted or rewritten to use with most other tools.

The following section gives a list of the most commonly used magical tools.

The Athame

I am starting with this one because it is the major implement utilised by witches and is used to cast the circle, summon the quarters, and consecrate water, salt, food, and drink. Some people assign it to the element of fire because, in the past, blades were almost always forged. Some allocate it to air because knives and swords represent the precise and cutting qualities of the intellect. The handle of the knife is traditionally black, but go with what suits you. Most athames are made of steel with a wooden handle. However, they can be carved entirely from wood or be made with a copper, brass, stone, bronze, or even silver blade. One of the most effective and beautiful athames I have seen was made from a sliver of obsidian and bound with thongs to a twisted driftwood handle. The handle itself can be carved or plain (I have seen two splendid and opulent examples with bronze blades, the handles embellished with semiprecious stones and carved from bone in the forms of goddesses). The blade can be unadorned or else engraved with patterns or symbols, including traditional Wiccan signs or astrological or planetary glyphs.

Athames can be crafted for the purpose, either sold ready-made or created to your own design and specification. Sources for these include pagan fairs and conferences, some occult and new age shops, and pagan online stores on the Internet. An alternative is to buy a kitchen knife or a sheath knife and then decorate and personalise it yourself, as many people do—but don't forget to blunt the blade or you will risk endangering yourself and your fellow celebrants. It is possible to pick up suitable looking knives from antique shops and junk stalls, but beware if you do this—you have no way of knowing how a knife was used before you found it, and you may be introducing unpleasant energies into your ritual space if you employ it there.

I used to be extremely uncomfortable with the concept of using a knife in the circle because of its connotations of cutting and bloodshed, and always cast the circle with a wand. I knew that the athame is never used to cut anything—only to direct energy—but my aversion remained. Then I saw a stall selling athames at a pagan fair and found myself picking one up. I was taken by surprise by the surge of energy that leapt from the blade, the sensation of power being channelled from the air around me and from all my chakras at once, though I wasn't consciously directing it. The thing felt alive, vibrant. I knew that using a wand would be tame in comparison from now on. Furthermore, I also realised that a knife that wasn't made for the purpose of cutting has no murderous or injurious intent attached to it.

Finally, if you are in a position to choose your athame in person—as opposed to ordering by mail or online—then go for the one that seems to call to you. Even knives of similar design are different and only one will be "yours," intended for you. Making this choice is likely to be intuitive rather than intellectual. Just trust your impulse and don't think too much when you decide. Don't worry if you do have to order "unseen"—things have a way of working out so that you get what is meant for you.

Very ceremonially minded groups also use a sword for casting the circle.

The Wand

The wand is ruled by either air or fire, according to your learning and preference. It can be used as an alternative to the athame to cast the circle, and is also employed to direct energy into other objects while working magic. Wands can be made of almost any wood, but certain trees have particular magical or mystical connections and are therefore suited to different purposes. Willow is a wood belonging to the Goddess and having a watery, psychic quality, making it good for all purpose wands, and is soft enough to carve easily—my own first wand was made from this wood. Oak is very masculine, powerful, and strong. Both rowan and hawthorn have properties of protection and a special magical essence. I once made a wand from a branch of hawthorn that had been torn down in a gale, and it made a particularly potent ritual tool—directed energy seemed to blast through it! The last two woods mentioned, rowan and hawthorn, are difficult to fashion because they are very hard. Hazel is another lovely wood to use and carries a bright, light, airy feel; it is very useful for spells concerned with mental creativity or intellectual development. There are other woods to consider and many books that go into detailed descriptions of their properties and purpose. I have only mentioned the ones I have used myself.

Wands can sometimes be found in shops and at fairs, but these are usually quite expensive. It's far better (and not very difficult) to make your own. Personally, I don't like cutting branches from a living tree, so all my wands have been made from fallen wood. An interestingly twisted root or piece of driftwood could be an alternative. I have always fashioned mine during a waxing moon to put the energy of growth and increase into them, but if you need a wand specifically for work on banishing unwanted conditions from your life, then it would be better to make it during a waning moon.

Find a quiet place where you can be comfortable and undisturbed. Handle the wood a bit before you start; it will help you to tune into the inherent essence and to get a feeling for how to work it. As you craft your wand, remain open and sympathetic to the nature of the tree from which it came, that way it will retain that spirit. Cut it to a comfortable length—about the length of your forearm is a good guideline—then cut off any twigs and either smooth them back or leave interesting looking knobbles. You can remove the bark or leave it intact. If you choose to remove it, the underlying wood can be sanded to a beautiful, smooth finish that can later be oiled. The shaft of the wand can be carved and set with small crystals or stones or just left plain to display its natural patterns and contours. I have set a crystal into the tip of each of my wands (with super glue, I'm afraid . . . probably not a sympathetic substance, but nothing else holds as well), and I have wound a spiral of copper wire round the crystal and onto the shaft to better concentrate and direct energy. One wand has a twining snake, which has been stained with colour, burned around the shaft with the point of a soldering iron; another has small pieces of amethyst and citrine embedded in its length; others are unadorned because the grain of the wood is beautiful enough on its own.

Despite my detailed instructions on wand making, I hardly ever use a wand myself during ritual. The athame does most jobs a wand can do and sends out a more concentrated focus of power. However, wand making is fun and satisfying, and a circle cast with a wand has a wonderful fiery softness and warmth that can be welcome at times when you want a quiet, relaxing rite.

The Cauldron and the Chalice

These two vessels belong to the element water and are symbols for the womb of the Goddess. I've always felt this to be slightly inappropriate since the womb is a closed organ, more like the shaman's crane bag, whilst the cauldron and chalice bear more resemblance to the pelvic girdle. However, the symbolism is traditional and seemingly dates back to extreme antiquity so should be respected. Because they are both containers, the connotations connected with them are of nurturing, gestation, and birth, and these ideas can be tied in with the development of spells and the unfolding of spiritual, psychological, and emotional growth and rebirth. In Celtic times the chalice and cauldron were connected with regeneration, and there are wonderful highly decorated examples to be seen in books and museums.

The chalice is mostly used to contain wine, juice, or spring water to be consumed at the end of a ritual. The contents are usually consecrated or blessed in some way that implies sacred sustenance or a libation; this custom has continued through classical Greek and Roman times and Christianity, and forms a central theme to the Arthurian legends.

The chalice our group uses is large, plain, and made of brass. I am not sure of the wisdom of drinking acid liquids like fruit juice or wine from a brass container, as I believe they have can have a corrosive effect on the metal, though none of us has been poisoned yet! My own personal chalice is silver plated and was picked up secondhand on a market stall. Chalices don't have to be made of metal; glass or pottery is perfectly acceptable, though it is fragile enough to be inappropriate for large circles. One of the nicest chalices I have seen was carved from a section of discarded oak gatepost. Moira, my coven sister, has one made from faience blue pottery, which she bought in Glastonbury; Robin's is made of pewter.

We were lucky enough to find our cauldron on the market. It was coated with rust and dirt and was therefore very cheap, despite being probably two or three hundred years old. They can also be found in antique shops for a price; reproduction cauldrons can be bought from occult and new age stores. Many new or renovated cauldrons have been treated with black lead, so be extremely cautious, as anything brewed in these will poison you!

Some groups place the cauldron in the centre of the circle and use it as the focus for ritual, a representation of Spirit. My group fills the cauldron with appropriate flowers, fruit, greenery, or candles at the festivals. I always place my spell candles in my cauldron and leave them there over the period of time it takes for them to be regularly relit and extinguished till they have burned right down and the spell is set. A cauldron makes a good fireproof container in which burning candles can be safely left. It also looks gorgeous with water and floating candles.

The Pentacle

This is round, flat, and usually about six inches in diameter. Simple ones have only a pentagram inscribed on the face, but more complex ones have additional symbols—often the signs for the three degrees of Gardnerian/Alexandrian Wicca. Pentagrams can be made of copper, brass, wood, ceramics, silver, and any other substance that can be shaped appropriately. Mine was designed by me and the design acid etched by my husband onto a circle of sheet copper; he put the same motif onto a round of cherry wood for himself. Pentacles are easily found through the same sources as other ritual equipment.

The pentacle belongs to the element of earth and so is used as a resting place for objects that need to be protected or rooted into the material plane within the circle. It's quite common to place the water and salt bowls on the pentacle during consecration, and the same is done whilst blessing food at the end of the ritual. I often put candles or cords on mine prior to using them in spells.

The pentacle is an important tool in the Craft because it bears the sign associated with present-day paganism, the pentagram, which combines the four elements and the sense of spirit or the psychic realms within its five points. This is an emblem of protection as well as being an image taken up by the earth religions as their badge (though it probably has its origins in ritual magic).

Censer, Incense, Herbs, and Oils

The censer and accompanying incense are ruled by the element of air; they are used to purify sacred space and to create mood and atmosphere as well as to obtain magical results. We have several censers, one of which is an opulent 1920s brass censer with a three-legged tray incorporated into its structure . . . this sounds rather vulgar, but in fact is very useful as the tray makes it possible for one to carry the lit censer round the circle without the danger of getting burnt. Another is made of pottery, and we have several metal bowls, shells, and so forth that can also be used. Lighted containers need to be placed on a fireproof surface such as a tile and should not be touched with bare hands—try it and you will find out why!

Although joss sticks can be used within ritual, loose incense is preferable as it is purer and smells much better. This is burned on little round self-igniting blocks of charcoal. Don't put the incense on till the charcoal is ash white and glowing all the way across or it won't burn very well.

Different types of incense have different properties and uses in ritual and magic. Frankincense has a clean, flowery and fruity smell. It can be used to purify a room and will cleanse it of all negativity, leaving a fresh, sparkling aura as though everything has been washed under a waterfall. It is a solar incense and really does bring in the sensation of being bathed in liquid light. Myrrh, on the other hand, is sombre, dark feeling, and very lunar and feminine; burning it brings in peace and healing. Benzoin, sacred to Venus, is sweet, musky, and erotic. All three of these are used as a base for the sort of incense you can buy in little glass jars from occult shops. There are many other incenses available, such as sandalwood, damiana, and copal. Each can be burned alone or mixed together, producing different moods and effects. Experimentation will help you to find your own favourites.

Some of the composite incenses, such as Isis, are lovely to use. You can also mix your own, buying the ingredients from herbalists and trying various combinations. Flowers, herbs, oils, and spices can be added to the mixture. Culinary mixed spices, for instance, are appropriate for Yule incense. Be careful, though, because some things that smell good when fresh are horrible when dried and lit; we tried throwing lemon balm on our Beltane bonfire one year and nearly asphyxiated everyone with clouds of thick white acrid smoke. It's a good idea to sit in quiet meditation and tune in to the feelings evoked by each new fragrance so you can gain some idea of the uses it can be put to. Be alert to which moods or symbols it suggests to you.

Various herbs can also be burned in ritual. Vervain smells like meadow hay and is very purifying and uplifting; it was sacred to the druids and was also used to cleanse Roman temples. Lavender is purifying and is calming as well. Rose petals give a sense of well-being. Native American smudge sticks, containing bundles of sage, cedar, and lavender are available from some occult shops and mail-order outlets and are used to purify one's space and aura.

Essential oils can be mixed with incense or evaporated over a candle flame in an oil burner. For people who are allergic to incense smoke, the latter can be a boon. Try geranium for protection, uplifting, and well-being, lavender for peace and purification, bergamot for happiness and to dispel depression, patchouli for centring, and cinnamon for a sparky, warm kind of energy. The last two, patchouli and cinnamon, are also used in money and prosperity spells.

These are a few of the resins, oils, herbs, and spices that can be used in ritual work. As with everything else in witchcraft, a lot depends upon your own perception and preferences, and since smell is the sense most connected to memory, certain associations will become attached to specific odours. At one time, I used to attend rituals with people who almost never used anything but benzoin: it was a long time before I could smell that particular incense without inadvertently conjuring up the details of their living room and ritual equipment. Now I use benzoin at Beltane and associate it with hawthorn and apple blossom.

The Altar

The altar can form a focus for the ritual because it holds flowers, food, candles, and your magical tools.

Witches' altars can be custom-made or can be makeshift temporary affairs such as a coffee table or chest covered with a cloth for the duration of the rite. Whatever is used will, of course, build up an aura of power, so if you don't want this energy permeating your everyday living space, you may want to make something to be used for ritual only. We have two altars: one that is large and rectangular and one that is an irregular slice of tree. Both are made of oak that we brought with us from our house in Brittany when we moved back to England. The big one is used for larger gatherings while the smaller one is used when there are no more than four of us.

If you are going to make an altar from wood, then please be conscious of the sources that are available. It is neither moral nor ecologically sound to use woods from the rain forests or other regions that are becoming deforested. As part of an earth spirituality, witches should be especially aware of the consequences of exploiting nature. Recycled wood is a different matter; it is perfectly acceptable to use Victorian mahogany, for instance, and this can often be picked up very cheaply or rescued when it has been thrown away (though remember to ask for permission before taking). Native woods are probably best, as they are in keeping with the spirit of the region in which you are living. Make your altar during a waxing moon and dedicate it before use.

There are many ways of laying out the altar. Everybody seems to have a different preference. Being quite methodical, I evolved my own layout by more or less placing things in the directions that match their elements. I place the chalice on the left and western side of the altar, censer and athame in the east, wand in the south. After this the directional correspondences break down. I put the pentacle in the centre because earth is the central element in witchcraft . . . and because it is easily accessible there for reaching objects I have put on it, such as food or materials for spells. The altar candles are at the back with the Goddess on the left (feminine) side and the God on the right (masculine); between them is a vase of flowers, corn, or greenery (whatever is appropriate for the specific ritual). The water bowl and salt box are at the front. Sometimes I also put a god or goddess figure somewhere on the altar as well.

The altar itself can be placed in the north, the sacred direction in witchcraft. When we work in mine and Nick's space we have to put the altar here as the layout of our room makes it impossible to place it anywhere else. Some people prefer to put it in the middle of the circle to make a central focus, and this is what we do if we work in Robin's home or outside. A couple I know put theirs in the east because they have a fireplace in their northern wall. Yet again, do what is right for you given your own circumstances and desires.

Candles

Candles are used on the altar, to mark the four quarters, and in some spells. The quarter or point candles are usually the colour of each element respectively, though some people prefer to place white candles in appropriately coloured glass jars. We use yellow for air (east), red for fire (south), blue for water (west), and green for earth (north). You can also stick to plain white. Some traditions use blue for air, green for water, and yellow for earth . . . it can be confusing, and only research, reading, and instinct can help you sort out what you prefer. I have stuck with the colour correspondences I first learned, partly because they seem right to me and partly because they are in common use and therefore are less likely to cause bafflement when I work with people outside my own group.

Altar candles are usually white and represent the Goddess and God. Variations include black for the Goddess and white for the God, green for the Goddess and red for the God, or even silver for the Goddess and gold for the God to represent the sun and moon (this analogy will not be appropriate if you assign masculine qualities to the moon and feminine to the sun, as do some Nordic traditions); you will find the combination that feels right to you. It is best to use one special holder for each. After a while, objects used in ritual really do take on the vibrations of the use to which they are put, and the circle stays more harmonious if these vibrations are not mixed up.

The colours for candle spells are discussed at length in the section on magic so I will not go into them here. Always use a fresh candle for each spell so there is no confusion of energies, otherwise the work will be distorted.

Newly bought candles need to be cleansed before being used in ritual work. I hold them in my hands and visualise them bathed in pure white light while saying, "May these candles be cleansed of all negativity that they may burn with the pure essence of the element of fire." After that I put them away in my candle chest. Just prior to using them I consecrate them through the four elements, whilst in the circle, passing them through incense smoke, saying, "I consecrate Thee with air," then candle flame, "I consecrate Thee with fire," then rubbing them with water, "I consecrate Thee with water," then salt, "I consecrate Thee with earth." Performing these actions ensures that other people's thoughts and energies, picked up during manufacture and transport, are effectively removed and cannot interfere with the candles' sacred use. Aside from that, consecrating any-thing through the elements balances it.

Any holders that appeal to you can be used to support candles, but they should be kept only for ritual use and not swapped around.

One last point: if you use candles and incense in your liv-ing space, you will have to be prepared for the fact that the smoke will discolour your walls and ceiling to a certain extent, though this will happen gradually over time.

Energy Raisers

The three major energy raisers in ritual are the drum, the voice, and the body itself.

Drums raise a huge amount of energy very quickly. My preferred drum is the Celtic bodhran, a round flat hand drum made of goatskin and played with a double-ended beater. The bodhran gives a high, full sound reminiscent of wild spaces and the running feet of animals. They can be acquired from music shops and festivals. One of mine was ordered by mail directly from the drum maker. They lend themselves very well to decoration with paints or inks and can be seen in abundance at pagan festivals, usually adorned with Celtic knotwork around the rim or across the skin. Moroccan and African drums are also very popular. Another way of producing percussive sounds is by clapping or beating the hands rhythmically. This can be almost as effective as drumming if done by a large group. Of course, any other musical instrument can help to raise energy.

Chanting or singing is also a good energy raiser; begin slowly and become faster and more melodic, or begin with low, regular sounds that accelerate into wild shrieks (this is better done in outdoor rituals rather than indoors in the proximity of curious neighbours!). You don't necessarily have to have specific words, just spontaneous sound will do. Large groups will find it easier to shed their inhibitions sufficiently to allow the vocalisation to develop.

Finally, circling, dancing, rotating, and spiralling in a clockwise direction are all good ways of raising power if you have the space. You can join hands and circle round and round whilst chanting, or dance the spiral dance—for which you need several people, one leading the others in an inward then outward spiralling snake. This kind of ritual dance has its roots in our pre-Christian past.

Cords

Tying knots in a length of cord is a way of fixing a spell. The usual number of knots is nine (a number of the Goddess), and the idea is to concentrate on the purpose of the spell as each knot is tied. I will explain this more fully in the section on magic.

If you like, you can use different coloured cords for different purposes: I use green or gold for money or prosperity, deep blue for spiritual work, white for peace and purification, red for anything requiring a boost of determination or power, and so on. The best cords are the thick braided ones used for upholstery; they can be found in many fabric shops. The length used should be a multiple of or a measurement of three (for the Goddess whose number this is), for instance, nine inches or three feet.

Cords are also worn by Alexandrian witches to show the level or "degree" of initiation that they have attained.

The Broom

This piece of equipment is optional. It is used to sweep round the room prior to casting the circle. This is a symbolic cleansing designed to remove psychic garbage, but the sound of the broom is quite hypnotic and relaxing and therefore serves to induce a calm and meditative state of mind, which begins to distance one from the everyday world and prepare one for ritual.

Traditionally, a witch's broom is made of birch twigs bound with willow to an ash handle. In practice it is extremely difficult to bind the broom using willow because it slips and breaks, so twine is a good substitute. Alternatively, you can buy a besom from a shop specialising in house or gardenware.

Clothing

Some individuals and groups work naked (or *skyclad*, as it is called by Wiccans), some wear robes, and some wear their everyday clothes.

Having been part of an initiatory Wiccan coven at one time, I am perfectly comfortable working without clothes. After the initial brief self-consciousness, it all feels matter-of-fact and normal and puts everyone on an equal footing. Really and truly, when unclothed, everyone has their own beauty and, conversely, nobody has a totally perfect body. Furthermore, being naked with others makes you very at home with yourself; nothing can be hidden and so body hang-ups and defences are easily discarded. It is sometimes claimed that clothes interfere with the free flow of psychic or magical energy, but I have never found this to be true. Taking ones clothes off for ritual is a choice; it should not be forced on people, nor should anyone be made to feel inferior or rejected if they wish to remain clothed.

Some groups and individuals wear robes, and indeed a garment worn only for ritual soon absorbs the vibration of the circle so that merely putting it on can induce the right frame of mind for magical work. Robes can be plain or embroidered and in whatever colour appeals to you. I used to wear a long black Indian dress, but some people have hooded robes that have been made for them or bought from occult suppliers. The main thing is to find something that is loose enough to be comfortable (and warm, too, if you are going to work outside in winter), but that has tight-fitting sleeves and is flame-retardant for safety around candles.

The group I work with wear ordinary clothes, but we take off our shoes before entering sacred space if we are indoors. I can't explain why the bare feet, except to say that it instinctively seems right . . . a feeling shared by many religions and spiritual paths around the world and throughout history. I still work skyclad when I am on my own; I like the sense of freedom and take pride in my naked form.

As with other articles reserved for ritual use, jewellery worn only in the circle soon acquires a strong psychic build-up, and therefore contributes to the frame of mind needed for magical work. Pendants are most commonly worn and can take the form of a pentagram, an Egyptian ankh, a Cretan labrys or double axe, a goddess or god form, crystals, and so on. Of course, most of these can be worn outside the circle as well. Wiccan high priestesses sometimes wear a silver bracelet.

A form of jewellery normally only worn in the circle, and only by female witches, is the witches' necklace. This is made of alternating amber and jet beads to represent light and dark, or of just plain amber. In initiatory Wiccan covens, only a second or third degree witch is allowed to wear such a necklace, but outside of this system there is no reason why any female witch should not wear one (I have never seen a male witch wear one . . . but why not?!). If you buy the beads separately and make the necklace yourself, cleanse the beads in water and sea salt for several hours to get rid of any psychic gunk and other people's vibrations that they will have accumulated. A lot of amber and jet is Victorian and will have passed through many hands on its way to you, so cleansing is extremely important.

Be aware that if you choose to wear jewellery for ritual, symbols are potent and attract and give out vibrations in tune with their own meaning and purpose. I wear a pentagram nearly all the time and I really do feel slightly less earthed if I take it off. I'm not sure how much of this feeling is due to the fact that I *believe* it is earthing me, but the end result is the same.

Tools of Divination

Among these are objects used for scrying; that is, gaining divinatory information by gazing into a shiny surface until the rational mind is lulled and insights arise. This is not my chosen method of divination—my professional work is done with tarot. However, within the confines of sacred space, I find that my ability becomes more acute. There is something about candlelight and being tuned into lunar power that lends itself to scrying.

I have a beautiful crystal ball made from a sphere of quartz. I also have a black witches' mirror (available at occult stores); this induces the right frame of mind very quickly because the colour and curve of the glass makes you feel as if you are gazing into fathomless space, and with no reflections to fix on, the mind disengages. Sometimes we pass a bowl of water round the circle for everyone to take a turn, and this is effective, too. In ancient times, polished metal mirrors were used. The first time I used my witches' mirror, I suddenly found myself catapulted into what I can only assume was spontaneous recall of some prior lifetime (it definitely felt like a memory, though I can't be absolutely sure). I felt extremely hot and was aware that my hair and face were soaked with sweat. I was gazing into a polished bronze mirror, holding the handle in one hand. I was looking at images of battle—there were horses and a lot of dust—and I was relaying what I saw to someone whom I was aware of as being with me but out of my field of vision.

The way to scry is to sit relaxed and comfortable and gaze into the crystal, mirror, or bowl, letting the eyes defocus slightly. When you first try, nothing much may happen, but if you persevere over a period of time you will get results, though these may only be impulses or feelings. Some people see pictures in the actual surface of the scrying tool. I see pictures, too, but these are in my mind's eye, though they are still vivid and accurate.

Tarot cards and runes can be employed in the circle, but they are less easy to read in candlelight. Personally, I also find them to be tools more suited to the intuitive than to the clairvoyant faculties, and, therefore, better read in daylight or electric light. This is my own slant. I'm sure many people would disagree with me.

Whatever method you use for gaining insights, always remember that nothing is fixed and immutable and that divination gives guidelines only. The value of using things like tarot or a crystal ball is that they can help to shed light on a situation or give useful intimations or probabilities that can then be worked with to change circumstances or bring deeper knowledge.

The Book of Shadows or Magical Journal

This can be an actual book or can be composed on a computer or word processor. It is used to record your rituals and spells, pathworkings and meditations, and any significant dreams that you remember (write them down when you first wake up: they will be fresh in your mind then. It's amazing how quickly they slip away after that).

At one time, I religiously wrote down everything immediately after it happened. It helped to fix it all in my mind and was great fun to read through. Now I hardly ever bother, partly because of laziness and lack of time and partly because I use a lot of spontaneous matter in my rites and can never remember exactly what I said and did once the candles are snuffed and the circle is opened.

Having said all that, I still think keeping a record of what you do is extremely important when you first start out. If I read back through my first Book of Shadows, I can trace how I gradually evolved my own style from the many other sources I had encountered. I wrote and adapted, then readapted as I found what was appropriate for me and what felt awkward or alien. Looking back now, I can also see how instructive some of my dreams were at that time, as they were filled with signs and symbols very pertinent to witchcraft.

If you go for an actual book, find one that appeals to you and invites you to write in it. The usual colour for a Book of Shadows is black, but really you can use any colour you want. My first one had a green marbled cover and gold-blocked page edges, and I kept it in green pen. I stuck pressed flowers from rituals in it and drew pictures. Because it looked pleasing, it encouraged me to use it. Black ink in bold pen strokes would be a good idea if you want to read your spells and rituals in the candlelit circle. If you keep yours on computer, find a font that appeals to you.

Gardnerian/Alexandrian witches are given their initiator's Book of Shadows to copy (a practice said to go back in history, though this is generally thought now to be legend rather than fact).

Ritual to Dedicate an Athame

Do this ritual some time between the new and full moon. You will need flowers for the altar, a bowl of water (preferably spring water, mineral water, or water from a sacred site), sea salt, ritual tools, incense, food, and something to drink.

Set up and cast the circle as usual, using a wand, your finger, or a crystal if you don't have an athame already.

Raise energy and call in the Goddess and God.

Pick up your new athame and pass it through the incense smoke, saying, "I consecrate Thee with air." Repeat using the other elements in turn, saying the words of consecration for each.

Now cradle the athame to you, imbuing it with your essence, infusing it with love, before saying, "May you serve me in rituals of sun and moon, in rites of seasonal celebration. I dedicate you to work between the worlds in the service of the Goddess and the God."

Go to the eastern quarter, hold out the athame, and say, "May you be filled with clarity and truth."

Go to the south and say, "May you be filled with intuition and inspiration."

In the west, say, "May you be filled with compassion and humility."

Finally, in the north, say, "May you be filled with productivity and integrity."

When you have finished, hold up the athame in salute to the northern quarter, kiss the blade, then cast a circle with it, thus forging your bond with the knife and between it and the sacred and magical powers of the circle.

Put the tip of the athame in the chalice and bless the liquid.

Do the same with the food, then feast and open the circle.

This is a very simple ritual but it contains the basic ingredients you need and can be embellished and adapted to suit your own tastes.

....

M
A
G
I
C
A
L

E
Q
U
I
P
M
E
N
T

CHAPTER EIGHT

Beltane

The garden is a froth of pink, white, and mauve blossoms, and
the breeze brings the scent of lilacs into the house. Comfrey and
honesty crowd the withered heads of daffodils; bluebells and vio-
lets are beginning to flower; tiny splotches of azure show where
the borage is reviving. Our apple trees are decked out in their
bright, pale wedding finery in honour of the Lady and the Lord.
The holly trees are splashed with acid green where new leaves
have overlaid the dark winter foliage. There are butterflies everywhere, yellow or blue or copper-brown. Magical blossom,
creamy and delicate, smothers the hawthorn hedges by field and
roadside, drenching the air with heady perfume. Rabbits scamper
in the sunny fields and blackbirds sing. The whole world seems

intoxicated with the joy of this most enchanted of months as spring opens out into summer.

When we leave the house at dawn, a half moon is hanging in the sky. It is still chilly, but the growing light has that milky luminosity only seen at this time of year, and which promises heat. As we near the city, other people join us, a steady stream heading for Magdalen Bridge to hear the choir greet summer.

At the Plain, I feel the earth energies strongly, as I always do; a feeling that grows stronger as we pass the grassy roundabout with its mistletoe-decked trees, then approach the bridge via water meadows. This usually busy thoroughfare is trafficked only by pedestrians this morning, and we have to step over several prone students in dinner jackets or ballgowns. The tradition of May Eve revelry has never died here in Oxford. A handsome drunk who is half my age staggers up and propositions me and I greet him cheerfully, amused and slightly flattered by his advances.

Chestnut blossom burns like candles through wreathing river mist. In a punt below the bridge a couple in evening dress hold real candles and swig champagne from a shared bottle. The bridge itself is packed, but from time to time the crowd parts to let through the naked young men who want to leap from the parapet into the Cherwell. Some years these foolhardy leapers are injured, but it never stops others taking their place next May Morning.

A hush descends on the crowd as the first rays of sunlight breach the treetops in the Botanical Gardens opposite us to strike Magdalen Tower, firing the old stonework to gold. At this signal, black and white banners are flung from the top of the tower where the choir boys have begun their Latin Hymn to the Sun, the annual welcoming of summer.

Afterward, we follow the rest of the crowd as it meanders down the High Street toward the city centre. By the Radcliffe Camera, Morris Men (traditional folk dancers) are dancing, *coloured ribbons flouncing, bells ringing . . . a higher sound than the pealing of Magdalen College bells, which resounds through the streets behind us. A strange pyramid of leaves looms out of the mist that still obscures the cobbles of the Turl—we know this is a man inside a wire support covered with leaves, but that doesn't take away the magic of meeting this human representative of the Green Man. Behind him, laughing men and women take their turn to frolic drunkenly round the maypole, which an elderly man is holding. All around us people are laughing, dancing, playing drums or pipes or fiddles, holding up children to get a better view. The city is giddy with May madness.*

By eight o'clock the sun has risen high in the sky and the air is heavy with increasing heat. We make our way home again whilst the rest of Oxford rises and prepares for the working day.

Later, in our garden, we drag the table out and load it with flowers, a cauldron of floating candles and apple blossom, a white cake with a Green Man painted on with emerald food colouring, bagels, poppy bread, honey. When everyone has breakfasted, we erect our small maypole and attempt our yearly dance. Only the children know what they are doing, as they have learned at their school May Day celebrations over the years. The rest of us romp around in a glorious tangle of rainbow ribbons, arguing, laughing, tripping over each other. We don't care. We are letting our hair down and having a huge amount of unalloyed fun.

Afterward, we light the Beltane bonfire and take turns jumping; we jump in one direction to dump something we want to lose from our lives, back the other way to wish for something new . . . back and forth as many times as we want, jostling each other for a turn, but keeping a wary eye on the flames to see that they don't get out of hand.

When we've had enough of that, we sit on the grass and watch Sally's new man who has promised us a display of fire juggling. He makes a spectacular figure, tall and dark against the backdrop

*of pale blossom, the vivid orange of his flame-sticks matching the
orange Celtic knotwork of his teeshirt.*

*After he has doused his flaming brands, we light our candles
and I recall the night before, May Eve, when Robin, Nick,
Moira, and I met to celebrate the marriage of the Lady of Flowers and the Horned Lord of the Greenwood. We had cast our circle in the oak woods under the stars, strewing the ground with a
foaming mass of blossom and lighting green and orange candles
and fragrant benzoin. The Lady had come dancing into our
space, lifting our hearts with gladness, and we had welcomed her.*

*Moira had called to the God: "Lord of the Greenwood, Hawk
of May, swift moving stag, enfold us in your gentle, fierce
embrace, father, brother, healer, lover, friend." As she ended the
words, we all felt a strong presence enfold us and saw a rush of
dancing, spangled sparks. The Lord came in like a bird, feathered
cloak spread, then he was a deer, deep chestnut skin so satiny, so
fine, that the veins stood out as they do on a thoroughbred horse.
I wanted to touch him, and in my mind I felt the textured animal
hide dissolve and transform into a man's skin. I saw his antlers,
still partly sheathed in velvet and sprigged with moss. Moira
"saw" him too, but the men told us later they were aware only of
a blur of green-speckled bronze.*

Beltane is a cross-quarter fire festival and falls on the
evening and night of April 30 and the following day, May 1.
The sun is in the earth sign of Taurus. Beltane is sacred to
the Celtic fire god Bel, to the Goddess as Flower Maiden,
and to the Horned God. The traditional time to celebrate
would be all through the night of April 30 and the next
morning.

This is a fertility festival when animals and birds are
breeding and blossom is bursting out in abundance everywhere. It is a time of waxing creativity in all our lives. In

times gone by, when increasing the population and securing successors was an issue, everybody cavorted off to the woods; maidens were deflowered and marriage vows were suspended as people paired off with each other's spouses. It was symbolic of the mating of the Goddess and God and the growth of crops and herds.

This is the time to dance around the maypole, which is a symbol of both phallus and worldtree, the interweaving ribbons representing the intertwining of male and female energies, the universal dance.

In ancient times the fires in the community were put out, then a fire of sacred woods was lit in honour of Bel. Cattle and sheep were driven past this to purify them of winter diseases and ill health. You can leap the Beltane fire to purify yourself of unwanted "baggage," and then again for wishes.

All over Britain, Morris Men still dance to celebrate the Sacred Marriage, and May Queens, youthful representatives of the Goddess as bride, are crowned. The Green Man is portrayed by Jack in the Green (a real man dressed in a canopy of leaves). Originally, sacred springs and wells were believed to be especially healing during May and were bedecked with flowers—a custom that has come down to us as well-dressing. Hawthorn (for the White Goddess, the ancient Lady of Britain) is brought into the house on May Eve to purify the home and bring fertility. Crowns of apple blossom can be worn by young girls on May Day.

The whole month of May is sacred and joyous.

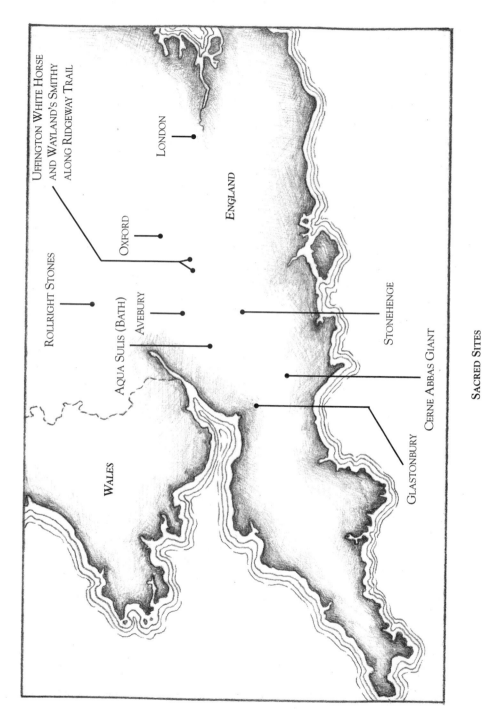

UFFINGTON WHITE HORSE
AND WAYLAND'S SMITHY
ALONG RIDGEWAY TRAIL

LONDON

ENGLAND

ROLLRIGHT STONES

OXFORD

AQUA SULIS (BATH)
AVEBURY

STONEHENGE

CERNE ABBAS GIANT

WALES

GLASTONBURY

SACRED SITES
(LOCATIONS ARE APPROXIMATE)

CHAPTER NINE

The Sacred Land

Everything is sacred—the whole earth and everything on it. But some places are power spots, concentrations of special energy. Sometimes you can feel these spots really strongly even though there is nothing that visually marks them as different. I have two areas in my garden like this, one of which feels comfortable yet energetic, and the other of which feels calm, feminine, and very mystical . . . a place where we sometimes practice moon rites because it feels like a gateway to the Otherworld. This type of power spot can be enhanced, as we found when we built a small stone circle at the bottom of our garden. We used eight stones, aligning them to the four major compass points and the cross-quarter points in between. When we had finished and dedicated the spot to the gods and the earth spirits, we were able to feel a definite increase of power. If you stand in the centre of the circle, it feels as if it is slowly rotating around you. Rituals performed there seem to flow and it is hardly necessary to cast the circle and summon the quarters—it is all already there. We constructed the circle whilst remaining intuitively aware of the energies present and the way they wanted to be channelled.

In prehistoric times people understood this. They constructed their sacred places where the earth energies were strong. They utilised all kinds of force, both masculine and feminine, active and passive, outward and inward flowing. If you go to any major stone circle and stand by some of the stones, you will feel yourself being energised by some and calmed by others. Furthermore, the level of force feels different at different times of the year, at the festivals, during different phases of the moon.

Going to a sacred site is a very good way to tune into the spirit of the land in which you are living. It will relax and replenish you and put you in touch with the local gods or ancestors, the legacy of the people who built and used the place. But if you do this you need to approach the experience with an open mind and be receptive to whatever comes to you there. There's absolutely no point arriving armed with crystals and shamanic rattles and proceeding to bang away, smudging and chanting in a manner stolen from a conglomeration of sources, none of which is attuned to this particular site or the culture it served. I'm not saying that drumming, chanting, and the like are inappropriate, but that they should arise spontaneously and as an expression of what is felt rather than being imposed out of preconceptions. Obviously, it may not be a good idea to indulge in vocal or percussive self-expression if there are other people around—you will be impinging on their enjoyment of the place, and, unless you are particularly brazen, you will feel like a prat. Worse still is the practice a few people have fallen into of burying large crystals in stone circles. If this has any effect at all it can only be detrimental: the original builders would have worked in sympathy with the flow of currents, so introducing any contrary energy could be seriously disruptive.

When you are exploring a sacred site, proceed calmly and respectfully, keeping all your senses open. Let the place speak to you, and don't try to apply modern conceptions to what you receive. Let it all work on you gradually. Take it into meditation or ritual when you get home if you like so you can increase your understanding. Trust your perceptions. I well remember being convinced that there was a crossing over of male and female currents at the huge stone circles at Avebury, an intuition that has been confirmed by many other people over the years.

Not all sacred sites are obvious. Some very old churches have been built on the sites of pagan temples, for instance. Many holy wells were once healing springs, and the original Celtic goddess or god is now masquerading as a saint. When we lived in Brittany, we had one such spring at the edge of our land. There was a chapel attached that was dedicated to a female saint. It was used once a year, at the Summer Solstice, when the local people arrived at the chapel to collect a statue of her saintly male partner (undoubtedly an echo of the Goddess and her consort), which would be paraded the short distance to the holy spring prior to riotous feasting and drunkenness. There are many other examples of such wells and springs, even in the centre of cities. Not all barrows and earthen temples are publicly known either, but sometimes you can see that a place has been enhanced by human endeavour, even though it may now have blended with the landscape. It is imperative that you never trespass on private land or invade space belonging to religious or spiritual communities, ethnic or otherwise.

Be sensible at sacred spots. There has been a great deal of damage in recent years; regrettably, some of it caused by a small minority of pagans. The Rollright Stones, for example, are now looked after by a group who want to protect and care for the circle whilst giving other pagans the opportunity to practice rituals there. Within reason, anyone can book the site for rituals or handfastings, yet people are sneaking in at odd times to use it and leaving splashes of candle wax on the stones, and chunks of stone have been chipped off and taken. I have seen candle stubs and cakes in foil containers (undoubtedly left as offerings) in the barrow entrance at Wayland's Smithy as well: this sort of residue is unsightly and will not biodegrade. Avebury has been disfigured with graffiti recently. Carnac in Brittany is now fenced off to stop people from climbing over the stones and doing untold damage in the process. The point is that if we abuse the privilege of having unrestricted access to these places, then we will lose it and will only be able to commune at a distance from beyond barricades.

My own experience of two visits to Stonehenge, thirty years apart, illustrates how devastating it can be to lose the right to enter a place that should be open to all of us unconditionally. The first time I went to Stonehenge, a whole group of us decided to make the journey from the West Country to Oxford. We drove up overnight in a convoy of the typically ancient and unreliable vehicles that you own when you are young and poorly paid, and were forced to spend what remained of the night in a barn because of engine trouble. It was too cold to sleep so just before dawn we got up and managed to fix the problem with the car. We realised we were near Stonehenge and decided to pay it a visit. The roads were empty except for dozens of rabbits as we approached through the misty early light. The stones were deserted when we reached them—apart from the rabbits and the cattle in a nearby field, there was no sign of life. It was a dancing place, filled with vibrancy overlaid with a sense of majesty. The circle itself does not cover a wide area but the stones are towering. We wandered around them at will, taking in the ambience. We felt as if we were breathing in rhythm with the heartbeat of old Britain. Sadly, we took the experience for granted, just a part of being young and exuberant. We piled into our vehicles and left the stones behind, forgetting them in the anticipation of the day ahead.

That was the last time I saw Stonehenge till recently, when four of us broke our journey there on our way back from Dorset. The route from the main road led us into a large carpark. It was a scorchingly hot day and the place was packed with people, many of them listening to portable audio guides or carrying informative pamphlets. An underpass led from the car park to the stones themselves. There were toilets, a cafeteria, souvenir shops, a ticket booth. The buildings were painted dark, drab green and looked like a military installation (in view of the violence and repression practised there during the Thatcher era toward people wanting to access the stones for celebratory purposes, the description is apt). We refused to pay the high entrance fee, particularly in view of the fact that the place belongs to the nation and should be free to enter, and instead sat at a bench drinking tea.

Then something happened that gave me some hope and fortified me for the subsequent walk across the road to take a closer look at the stone ring. Two or three crows and some starlings were perched on the perimeter fence near a patch of brambles; they were overlooking the burial mounds in the field beyond. As I idly watched the crows and battled with my anger and shock, I experienced a sudden shift in consciousness so that the birds, the brambles, and the landscape came into sharp focus whilst the tourist development faded back. I felt as though the land spoke to me—there is no clearer way to express the experience. I was told that the ugliness and commercialism would pass one day, more enlightened times would come, and the stones and the countryside around would still be there. That gave me a glimpse of hope that stayed with me as I pressed my face to the stout chain-link fence and watched people parade around the paths and raised walkways that contain visitors and prevent them from reaching the stones. The land around Stonehenge is still vital, but the stone ring itself has been capped off so that the energy is repressed. For thousands of British pagans, and for others across the world, the heart of their spirituality has been stilled. We heard quite a few other people complaining about the unattractive and inappropriate way the site is now managed, so we weren't the only ones affected.

There are hundreds of sacred places in Britain alone, some of which I will describe briefly in the following pages. I have deliberately refrained from going into historical or geographical detail but have instead stuck to the sort of perceptions that are relevant to spiritual exploration.

Uffington White Horse and Wayland's Smithy

These two places are connected by the ancient Ridgeway track. Uffington White Horse, a creature of fluidly drawn chalk lines, crowns the high point of the downs above the Vale of the White Horse in Oxfordshire. Nearby are Uffington Castle, an ancient earthworks, and the flat-topped, conical Dragon Hill. The White Horse is over 350 feet long and 150 feet high and can only be seen in its entirety from a distance. Close up, or from on the hill itself, it becomes a collection of dynamic abstract shapes. Here the land curves into rippling folds over which the windblown grass shimmers like water. It is a place where the spirits of earth and air meet and blend. The sky is vast, curving at the horizon to meet the plains below. Standing atop the White Horse, one feels a timelessness and freedom on which the twenty-first century barely encroaches (despite the presence nearby of a car park and attendant ice cream van).

Wayland's Smithy can be reached by a walk of about a mile along the Ridgeway from the White Horse. This walk is particularly evocative in spring when the hawthorn trees that flank the rutted chalk path are a mass of pink and white blossom. Wayland's Smithy itself, a long barrow shored up by towering megaliths, is set off the Ridgeway in a copse of beech trees amid corn fields. It is a place of patterned light and shade. On sunny winter days the bare branches of beech cast striped shadows across the barrow and its surrounding paths. The summer leaves filter spangled light and throw dappled coins across the grass.

The energy here is indescribable and constantly changing. It is earthy, feminine, soft yet fiery. The entrance to the barrow has been blocked, forming a cave just large enough to accommodate someone small curled in a fetal position.

Halfway down the length of the barrow, which tapers in both height and width, the veil between the worlds is extremely thin and it is possible to momentarily lose the connection with this level of being as the Otherworld impinges on consciousness.

Avebury

The whole of Wiltshire is covered with Neolithic remains, but Avebury is the largest. This site is huge, comprising a snaking avenue of massive megaliths that leads to a high manmade bank containing the remains of the stone circles. In the middle of the complex are the present-day village, church, and manor. Sheep graze among the stones and the whole place is sublimely peaceful, cradled as it is by the surrounding landscape of gently rolling farmland. West Kennet Long Barrow is nearby, and Silbury Hill rises like a great pregnant belly on the skyline.

It is a happy place, and walking around it lifts the spirits. The only part that contradicts this impression is near the church, where a lot of the stones have been destroyed; here there is a dark and angry atmosphere. Otherwise, tranquillity overlays a bubbling joyousness. The air is very clear and fresh. The stones seem to invite physical contact; the impulse to embrace some of them is overwhelming and it's easy to see why the stereotype of the stone-hugging neopagan hippie has arisen. Some of the megaliths feel maternal while some have a strong, vibrantly masculine resonance. Many of the stones have naturally formed but clearly discernible "faces," and are decorated with black disks of lichen.

Avebury comes alive at the eight points of the solar year, especially at Beltane and Lammas, so it seems reasonable to assume that it was once used for fertility and harvest rites. There is the overwhelming sense that this is a place built so people might interact with the Great Goddess, the Earth Mother who nourished and sustained them in life and took their bodies back into her womb at death.

The Rollright Stones

This is a small stone circle on the Oxfordshire/Warwickshire border in the middle of the Cotswold Hills. The ring, surrounded by pine trees, consists of very small stones, the tallest being only head height. They are irregular in shape, having twisted, almost human forms, and their surfaces are pitted with holes and covered with rounds of bronze lichen. Legend says it is impossible to count the stones . . . and indeed there are so many different sizes, including small fragments, that it is difficult to deduce what to include.

Across the road is a taller stone called the King Stone. There used to be a beautiful mature blackthorn bush here, but the farmer who uses the field cut it down because the litter caught in its branches was being consumed by his cows along with the leaves, thus putting them in danger of a blocked gut from swallowed packages and plastic food wrappers. The removal of the tree has destroyed some of the presence of the place.

A little distance up the road and across a field are the Whispering Knights, a group of stones that once formed the supports to an earthen burial chamber. These are surrounded by metal railings (as is the King Stone) but are clearly visible.

The whole Rollright complex is extremely mystical. It feels earthier and more intimate than Avebury, and at certain times the current of energy it gives off is electrifying. It has a long association with witchcraft, and many contemporary British witches have performed rituals there. This is another sacred site that has a vibration of fertility rites, especially at Oestara and Lammas.

The circle itself is privately owned and has recently been bought by a number of people who have collaborated to prevent it from falling into the hands of developers.

The Cerne Abbas Giant

The Giant can be viewed in his entirety from the side of the road that runs by his hill. He stands with feet planted firmly apart, left arm outstretched, right arm raised above his head brandishing a club whose wavy outlines are reminiscent of a deer's antler. His round head is bald; his navel and ribs are defined. His erect phallus is apparently thirty feet high, which, since it is reasonably in proportion with the rest of him, gives some idea of the scale of his whole figure.

If you visit the Giant in summer, you climb up past fields edged with chamomile. At the foot of his hill is a beech wood, a place of light and shadows, a sanctuary of soft, feminine energy overlooking a sunlit meadow at whose perimeter nestle barrowlike mounds.

As you climb the steep chalk paths, beeches give way to hawthorns, which in turn peter out, leaving the ground open to the sky. There, amid purple vetch, blue scabious, tiny yellow and orange ladies slipper, bright pink orchids, and a myriad of other wild flowers, butterflies dance up from under your feet. The side of the hill rises steeply so that it is almost necessary to pull yourself up on hands and knees. The Giant himself has been fenced off to prevent erosion damage and only one side of him can be glimpsed—a strange muddle of abstract shapes when viewed from so close. The village of Cerne Abbas can be seen from the top of the hill, as can many miles of the beautiful, dreaming Dorset countryside.

In bygone days, the hillside was the site of Mayday fertility rites. This is a place of serpent power. The energies of the earth writhe up to flood your auric field with vitality and light. There are real snakes here, too, for adders bask in the sun on hot days. It is worth the steep, sweaty climb for the boost of exhilarating, raw elemental force that floods out of the land.

No one seems sure if the Cerne Abbas Giant is Saxon, Celtic, or even older, or just a seventeenth-century joke. It hardly seems to matter. Whenever he was carved into his hillside, it was obviously in response to the masculine, creative flow of vital force there. Certainly, the villagers who once set their maypole in the earthworks above his head at Beltane must have recognised his fertility.

Aqua Sulis

This is the site of the Roman baths in the city of Bath. Several ages have imposed their identity so that you leave the shops of contemporary Bath to enter the Georgian Facade, passing the Pump Room to go down to the Roman temple of Minerva. At the heart of the complex is the original hot spring, which became a place of worship in Celtic times. As was often the case in countries colonised by Rome, the original local goddess, Sulis, was integrated with but not absorbed by the imposition of the Roman deity Minerva.

This site isn't free, but it is worth paying the entrance fee, battling through crowds of other people, and bypassing the computerised displays of tourist information. The Roman baths are now open to the sky, but the green water is hot and steam rises from it, carrying the smell of sulphur. The remains of the Roman temple are now underground, and you pass displays of coins, figurines, and, in one case, a strange flattened mask reminiscent of the gold Mycenian mask of Agammemnon.

On the stairs to the lower level is a huge stone facade displaying the carving of the head of a Romano-Celtic sun god with flamelike serpents intertwining with his hair and beard. This image is dynamic and powerful, yet, because the aura of the place is overwhelmingly feminine, the masculine force is not predominant. There is also a bronze bust of Minerva.

As you go deeper into the temple, you become increasingly aware of an energy that uplifts you at the same time as taking you deep within yourself. This feeling grows, enfolding you in quiet ecstasy, till you have finally reached a viewing platform overlooking the place where the hotspring gushes from the bowels of the earth, the water is mysteriously wreathed in steam, the surrounding rock is encrusted with sulphurous bronze and orange deposits. There are hundreds of coins in the pool below, where visitors have flung in offerings and made wishes. The sense of presence here is tangible. It is a place of fire and water, of solar power issuing from the earth. Everything within you seems to dissolve away, leaving only a sense of being without division or separation from whatever force lives here.

Later, as you leave, you will pass another, much larger pool, dank and chilly. Its bottom is covered with money of many different currencies. This is the only unpleasant part of the complex—even the ruined sacrificial altar has no apparent residue of pain or fear. Originally, people threw offerings here when petitioning Sulis to blight their enemies on their behalf. It is a repository for curses.

The experience of Aqua Sulis is chthonic and it would be unwise to underestimate the effect a visit can have. My dreams have been vivid and filled with underworld imagery and the symbolic evidence of the processing of subconscious material after going there.

Aqua Sulis is a particularly potent place around Imbolc, so there may be connections with Brighid, especially in view of the blend of the elements of fire and water here.

You can meditate on your experience of a sacred site once you return home, allowing yourself to remain receptive to whatever your intuition wants to tell you. Sometimes material surfaces spontaneously, as in the experience that I recount below, which happened during an unfocused meditation after a visit to Glastonbury.

Glastonbury Meditation

I sit in a half lotus. The room is dark except for one candle before me on my shrine. I breathe calmly, centring myself into my lower chakras, inhaling and exhaling as though through my stomach, letting everything go, opening to whatever thoughts and visions arise . . . not judging but just being one with whatever presents itself to me.

I become aware that I am seated on the ground, which is like a hollow opening out to cup me. A current of force starts to flow through me, beginning with my feet, buttocks, and perineum, and coursing up my spine till I am surrounded by golden dancing sparks. My body is a tree rooted at the bottom of Glastonbury Tor with roots going down into Chalice Well. All around me are apple trees. I see their blossom but at the same time smell their ripe fruit. I am not an apple tree myself but just the essence of tree.

The well at my roots is the womb of Glastonbury and its dreaming, watery presence pervades the town and shapes the consciousness of all who go there seeking spiritual truth. There are many answers and many ways—some of them misleading, some of them enlightening.

My body is dissolving, merging with the earth which is no longer solid, so that my body and earth body become one. Everything is opening out and blending, and my earthly form is no longer a barrier separating me from a wider reality . . . yet still my roots go down strong and sure.

Gradually, my form becomes solid again and human. I open my eyes and pat my legs to affirm my outer self, and am fully aware in the outer world once more.

I have described places that I have visited personally and that are meaningful to me. There are many others, both in Britain and around the world. There are also many, many sacred places that have never been enhanced but are natural spots, maybe hidden or maybe accessible to all. Some places make you want to visit them even though they do not contain megaliths or a temple. Sites that have been the scene of worship have become so because our ancestors recognised their special quality and built on or utilised them in some way, but there are many other places that are just as meaningful; places that have never been used for spiritual purposes, or places that were used so long ago that it has now been forgotten. A pool, a stream, an ancient tree—all can hold mysterious power or give out emanations conducive to revelation and magic. Trust your inner perceptions, go where you are guided, and walk lightly on the earth.

CHAPTER TEN

Full Moon

At the bottom of the garden, in the stone circle, we watch through the branches of the apple trees as the full moon comes up over the roof of the house. The sky is clear, not yet completely dark but smattered with stars. A bat flits and wheels, darting after airborne insects. The scent of honeysuckle is strong.

We light the point candles and place their protective jars in the four quarters. The moonlight, so strong in the rest of the garden, does not reach here, and the warm dark cavern formed by trailing willow is suffused with a dim orange glow against which our moving shapes are thrown into relief. The air is so still that the unshielded altar candles barely flicker and incense smoke weaves lazily, hardly releasing its fragrance of lavender, sandalwood, and rose. Moths hover at the edges of light.

When everything is prepared and the circle is cast, the quarters summoned, we join hands and gyrate round the central altar, dancing faster and faster till we are dizzy and laughing and breathless.

Then I stand with my upraised arms stretched toward the moon, feeling power stream through my fingers, twining snakelike down my arms, swelling, pouring, coursing through my body. I feel remote, distant, but at the same time incredibly present and real. Later, I will try to analyse the experience, and words and thoughts will fail; but for now, I just am and everything is complete, is rooted in this place, this moment. I had not planned how I would call in the Goddess, but the words of summoning seem to form without any mental effort: "O, Lady of many names, Great Mother, be with us now. Bring beauty and love, joy and fulfillment to the work we do tonight."

I lower my arms and step back as Robin speaks the words of summoning that call in the God: "Fierce Lord, Horned One, guide and protector, bring power and strength and truth to what we do."

The candle flames gutter and then are still. The circle seems less empty and is charged with power. We begin our magical working, each of us stating our intention in turn, going clockwise round the circle . . . the direction of increase. Moira wants healing for a friend, and as she states her intent we all concentrate on it, willing it to be, visualising the person well and strong. The friend has asked Moira to help, otherwise we would not be bringing the matter into the circle, for to do so without permission would be an infringement of this person's free will. Robin wants to find a means for himself and his wife to live together all week. At the moment they are working in different cities and only see each other during the weekends. Nick needs the confidence to break out of a rut and find a new job. He knows he constantly blocks himself and needs to find a way to *face his fear of change, and to value himself. I want the money to upgrade my computer so I can run the programmes I need for my creative work. Each wish is voiced and then empowered, till we have come full circle.*

Now we link hands again, beginning to draw up the energy in the circle, forming it into a swirl of crackling light and power that we push with our minds, each of us imagining our own and each other's stated wishes being woven into the fabric of this swirling, spinning vessel of force. Faster and faster it goes till it gains momentum, takes on independent life, rises higher; a cone of radiance like a unicorn's horn, its base our ring of outstretched arms, its tip high above our heads. Simultaneously, we experience the orgasmic point of maximum charge and together release our hands from each other's grasp. The spiral of power goes winging out into the night, carrying our wishes toward their realisation.

"Wow!" says Robin as we flop down on the ground. The space in the stone ring is empty now, the vitality used up. I feel drained but happy. Nick, who always has more pep than anyone else, says he feels spaced-out. Moira expresses the need to get back to her children soon. The time has come to bless food and drink and share our feast, an activity that will ground and revitalise us as well as draw us closer in the companionship of shared celebration.

Moira raises the chalice of white grape juice in blessing. Nick raises the pentacle of food and asks that its contents ground and nourish us. Then we are talking and laughing together, mundane matters creeping into the conversation, our everyday lives impinging once more as we share moon cakes and fresh apricots. Soon the experience of the ritual has faded back a little and we are ready to thank the Goddess and God, open the circle, and go our separate ways, though the shared occurrences of the last hour or so will stay with us all for some days to come, enriching our lives.

The moon is full when it is 180 degrees from the sun and in the opposing astrological sign; so, for instance, if the sun were in Cancer then the full moon would be in the opposite sign of Capricorn. The moon is considered to be full for magical purposes during the day before, the day of, and the day after it has waxed completely.

This is a time when spiritual and psychic forces are in full flood and the cosmic tides have peaked. When the night sky is clear, everything is bathed in celestial radiance as the moon reflects the stepped-down light and strength of the sun to us. But even when the moon is hidden by clouds or rain we can still feel its influence. Quiet activities like insight meditation become difficult; animals are more lively; people want to be out enjoying themselves; there is a restlessness and tension that can sometimes manifest in drunkenness and violence on city streets. Psychic awareness is at its optimum, and this is a prime time for spiritual work or magic. Full moon energy is only troublesome when it is unchannelled.

To witches, the full moon is the time of the Mother; the fertile phase of women's lives, from late puberty to just before the menopause, is ruled by her. Cycles of productivity peak at this time too, and magic worked now is concerned with bringing fully formed wishes into manifestation, rather than working on the development of new ones, and will more than likely be successful.

The full moon is also the optimum time to celebrate connection with the Great Mother and her horned consort, and pagan groups that meet only once a month will almost certainly choose to do so now.

For rituals at this time, put fully opened flowers, perhaps lilies or roses, on the altar. Appropriate incenses would include jasmine, lotus, and sandalwood. I sometimes light an ivory white candle on my shrine and burn it on the evenings and mornings of the three days of the full moon phase to honour the Goddess.

One way to understand and become fully attuned to this moon's phase is to do a meditation with the full moon as your focus. Sit somewhere quiet and in a position that is comfortable. Light a candle if you like. Tell yourself that you are protected and safe and that when the meditation is finished you will be grounded and alert. If you can see the moon from where you are, that can help, but it isn't essential. Look at the moon, or build up its image in your mind; see it hanging round and bright in the dark night sky, or low on the horizon at dusk. Relax and breathe in its light till it begins to suffuse your body with its silvery essence. How do you feel? What thoughts and pictures, if any, do you begin to experience? Remain aware of your material surroundings, your body, but let yourself be drawn deeper into the meditation. Don't try to force or anticipate anything, just trust your inner perceptions and allow yourself to follow them calmly. When you sense that you are ready, allow the images and feelings to recede, see yourself looking at the full moon once more, then pat your body to earth yourself. Write down the meditation in your Book of Shadows, put out any candles, and then have something to eat.

There are many examples of pathworkings in books. They lay down a script that you follow, telling you roughly what to see and how to respond. If you don't feel confident about allowing your own experience in visualisation, then by all means try one of these. I always hated them because they seemed to limit me and tell me what should happen to me. They are someone else's way of interpreting what should be deeply personal. However, I offer one of my own full moon meditations on the following page, which you can use as an example and to get a few "how to" hints. It was done some years ago when I was preparing for initiation.

Full Moon Meditation

It is Monday, the day of the moon, the 13, which is a Goddess number, and the moon is in its own sign of Cancer.

I sit on the patterned Native American rug in the bedroom and cast a bright circle of light round me with my mind. The sky is clear except for one or two streaks of cloud, so moonlight pours down and bleaches the roofs opposite my window. After a while the light seems dazzling, so I shut my eyes but can still see the moon's radiant disc.

Soon a landscape begins to form with wooded hills and a white track leading in. I am filled and surrounded with the most incredible sense of love; it moves me to exultant tears. As I make my way into the landscape, I can sense and almost smell amniotic fluid. There is a sense of imminent birth, as though the land itself could part to allow a newborn child to emerge.

With the woods behind me now, I walk along the track. It is chalk white and edged by rich green grass. Yellow flowers and then pink spring up by my feet as I pass. To my right is a magical tree like an apple tree with glowing round fruits, and beneath it, a spotted fawn lies. Ahead, the land swells into a green hill, bare except for a solitary standing stone like a pointing finger. It draws my attention upward, and I see that the sky is pale pink with the creamy coloured full moon huge and low on the horizon so that it fills almost my whole field of vision. Every crater and line on it stand out pale and distinct, but as I watch they fade back, melting into the shape of a hare, creature of the Goddess.

As my eyes return to the landscape, I see that there is a cave in the hillside now. I move forward to enter, knowing I am entering the body of the Mother. Inside is reddish dark, warm. I feel suddenly so centred and calm. I feel as a baby must feel in the womb: safe; connected, yet almost detached as well; content with just being, without conscious thought or motivation. Everything feels right.

Then somehow I am outside again, or maybe inside has opened up into further experience. I see bright emerald birch leaves (birch is the tree of birth) and sense a woman, very pregnant and with a crown of stars in her hair. Behind her I see the deep celestial blue, which belongs to Inanna and Isis and Mary.

I feel that I have come home; and as this thought forms I know the Goddess is leaving, centring herself back into my inner self. As she begins to fade, she turns her face one way and then the other, revealing her other selves, the Maiden and the Crone.

As I come back fully into myself and become aware of my normal surroundings, I am buoyed up by strength and wisdom and love.

CHAPTER ELEVEN

Summer Solstice

Hollyhocks tower by the back door, magenta, yellow, and cream. Bees hover industriously above the masses of old-fashioned roses then dive into red, pink, or butter coloured flower heads, emerging with bodies dusted with pollen. Butterflies sip nectar from cerise trumpets of mallow, then settle on the marigolds to sun themselves. On the pond, baby frogs sit poised on the flat round leaves and waxy white blooms of the water lily while brown dragonflies and turquoise damsels zoom over like biplanes. Small green apples nestle between twig and branch or lie under the trees from which they have dropped. Some days it rains, but the rest of the time the skies are clear, except for the occasional fat white clouds that build up and disperse while I watch from my summer place on the bench; and in the long light evenings, swallows swoop and

*circle with faint, peeping cries. The Otherworld feeling in my gar-
den increases as Midsummer approaches. The oak tree drowses,
confident in his power, but nearer to the house the Holly King
rattles his spiny leaves and prepares to do battle.*

*Out in the fields the corn is turning from green to gold and the
hay is being cut. Tree and hedgerow have lost their springtime
brightness and have faded back to a dusty dark green as everything in nature leaves behind its previous giddy vitality and settles
to the serious business of being productive. Cattle browse with
swelling flanks and horses stand head to tail to whisk the first of
the summer's flies from each other's faces.*

*Robin has gone away with his wife, so on the eve of the Solstice
Moira, Nick, and I drive out into the countryside to perform our
ritual without him. The place we have chosen is a clump of beech
trees that crown a hill, the haunt of picnickers and kite-flying children during the day. Tonight, by moonlight, it is a place of power
and beauty, brooding over the sleeping countryside. As we take
the hill path and enter the trees, we are enveloped in an aura of
hushed, yet expectant, stillness. The smooth trunks tower up,
white and mysterious; great twisted roots reach down into the
soil. Over the last two centuries, initials have been carved into the
bark, and those with Victorian dates have grown with the trees so
now they are wide and flattened and many inches high. Our foot-
falls are muffled by layers of leaf mould.*

*In the inner sanctum, a natural clearing at the heart of the
grove, we lay out candles and incense in sturdy containers. The
ground is damp from recent rain, but even so we have no wish to
risk causing fire damage. We sprinkle rose petals at the perimeter
of the circle then light frankincense . . . solar incense for a sun
festival. As the smoke rises, a pale shape emerges from the
branches overhead and drifts above the circle, startling us. An
owl. We laugh and relax again. A fox barks from somewhere
across country, setting off an answering clamour as a dog closer*

at hand takes up the challenge then falls silent. Fragrant smoke blends with the odour of damp earth. Sound and smell are accentuated and our senses are enhanced.

In our quiet space under the trees, we honour the Sun King, he who will soon start to fail as autumn approaches. We acknowledge the Oak King too, who must accept the challenge of the Holly King, his dark brother, his younger self. But at this moment we are approaching the dawn of the longest day and the peak of his power. We light a golden candle in representation of his glory.

The moon is setting as we start our feast of honey cakes and fruit. Some time later we pack up our ritual paraphernalia, then sit out on the open hillside at the wood's perimeter to wait for dawn. The increasing light picks out a thick white ground mist trapped in the folds of the landscape toward the river. As we watch, the mist turns first pink, then pale gold, and then the sun is breaking free of the horizon, its rim aflame. Moira raises the chalice in salute and the light flares along its lip briefly. As we drink, there is a moment of total silence . . . we hold our breaths in response. Then a bird begins to sing, followed by another until the trees behind us are alive with their music. The presence we felt but barely noticed during darkness, the soul of the land, gives way before the swelling of light, the vitality of daybreak.

The Summer Solstice is a solar festival and takes place around June 21 when the sun moves into the astrological sign of Cancer. Because Cancer is ruled by the moon, the ingress of the sun into this sign is akin to the marrying of masculine and feminine, Goddess and God. This is the longest day of the year. The sun is at the height of his power. The God is in his prime. After this, the days will begin to shorten and the nights to lengthen. This is the creative peak, the apex of the outward cycle of the year when our creativity begins to bear fruit as the crops ripen toward harvest.

Like Beltane, this is a time when bonfires can be lit to represent the sun's zenith, and at one time beacons would have been lit on hills throughout Britain. Now, the god of vegetation and grain prepares for his death at Lammas. The Oak King reaches his prime and must shortly give way to the Holly King, who will rule from now till Yule.

The Goddess is seen as the Earth Mother, her body bearing the ripening fruit and grain, but her fecundity has almost peaked and she gradually moves toward harvest and her winter death aspect when she will take the dying God back into her body to await his rebirth.

This is a relaxing, mellow festival. Roses are gathered and can be woven into a sunwheel, along with yellow and orange summer flowers. Soft fruits are in abundant supply and should form part of any feasting now.

CHAPTER TWELVE

The Circle

A cast circle is a sacred place, a barrier between the busy outer world and the world of spiritual expression, a container that keeps in power and keeps out everyday distractions. Within this space emotions and psychic awareness are enhanced, but sounds from beyond its confines are muted and seem far away—it is amazing how much cooler and noisier a room will seem once the circle has been opened again. The circle is the equivalent of the temple or church of other religions. However, unlike the rectangular layout of most religious meeting places, where one person of elevated status stands apart and guides a congregation through the service, the pagan or witches' circle is a space where everyone is equal and contributes fully to every part of the rite, and where the shape and layout preclude anyone enjoying a superior position—though one or more participants may go to the centre of the circle during the ritual and become a point of focus.

Although the pattern of "building" sacred space may vary between different branches of paganism, the ingredients are the same and fulfill the same functions, which are to cleanse, purify, protect, and enhance. Some people call in the quarters before they cast the circle and some construct the circle first, but the result on completion will be similar. There is no "set in stone" correct way to do all this. I have worked with Wiccans, hedge witches, druids, and "nondenominational" pagans, and the pattern of circle casting is almost the same in every case. Anyway, it is doubtful whether the witches of old practised within a circle at all; this is something probably borrowed from ritual magic, along with the pentagram, knife, and wand. The original village witches were healers and herbalists who very likely worked with a respect for the solar and lunar cycles (as did most folks then), but who also were probably not against handing out spells of cursing or procuring abortions, and who would be amazed to hear that their craft was a path to spiritual growth and self-realisation.

By creating the circle, we enact the pentagram, the basic symbol of witchcraft, because we use the four basic elements and directions and the central, fifth element of spirit, all of which the pentagram stands for. By performing ritual within that space we are touching the deepest part of ourselves, that which has no knowledge of separation.

It's best not to eat too close to doing ritual. Leave a gap of at least an hour and a half beforehand if possible, or you will feel heavy and clogged because food is earthing.

The sequence of circle casting which I use is:

- Set everything up.

- Bathe or wash prior to taking off clothes or putting on special garments.

- Light the point and altar candles and charcoal.

- Sweep the perimeter of the circle with the broom.

- Stand and quietly centre, letting go of the everyday world, breathing rhythmically, allowing the chakras to open.

- Sprinkle incense on the now glowing charcoal.

- Consecrate water and salt.

- Cleanse the perimeter of the circle and its occupants with salted water and then incense.

- Cast the circle.

- Call in the quarters.

- Raise energy.

- Call in the Goddess and the God.

- Conduct the purpose of the ritual.

- Bless food and drink.

- Feast.

- Bid farewell to Goddess and God.

- Open the circle.

Setting up

When I work on my own, I set up first so that I can be relaxed and refreshed from my bath and won't lose that serenity whilst bustling around laying everything out. In group rituals, everyone should share in setting up, and the sequence and rhythm of this then becomes part of the ritual and a way of preparing the mind and emotions.

Place the point candles in their appropriate directions (you can use a compass if you aren't sure) putting a yellow candle in the east, red in the south, blue in the west, and green in the north.

The altar can be placed in the centre of the circle or else the north. On it, put your athame, wand (if you want to use it), pentacle, censer, chalice with drink in, Goddess and God candles, flowers or other decoration or seasonal offer-ings, food, any articles used for magic (such as candles or cords for spellwork), a candle snuffer if needed, a statue of Goddess or God if desired.

If you want to sweep the circle, lay the broom somewhere close to you.

Bring out anything else you will be using, such as a caul-dron to contain candles or flowers or in which to place spells in progress. Make sure you have extra holders if you have candles for magical work. It is a nuisance to seal yourself into sacred space and do your ritual only to find that there is nothing in which to place your newly lit spell candle.

Purifying the Body

The concept of a ritual bath or wash is common to many religions and represents a removing of everyday concerns and a preparation for spiritual communion. It does *not* mean that the body is unclean or impure. In witchcraft, the body is sacred and we experience our spirituality through the physical world and nature just as much as through religious acts . . . the two are seen as inseparable.

A lovely way to cleanse the aura of unwanted vibrations and put oneself in a frame of mind ready for ritual is to put herbs and sea salt in the bath. The salt can be thrown in and allowed to dissolve, but the herbs are best tied into a piece of porous cloth and hung under the hot tap, otherwise they block the drain and leave a mess all round the bath. Some suitable herbs are lemon balm (not too much or it will make you sleepy!), rosemary, vervain, lavender, and chamomile. You can use them separately or mixed together.

As you lie in the bath, imagine your whole being washed clean of any impurities and stresses accumulated during the day.

Lighting Candles

I always light the point candles first, starting with the east and working round in the order in which the quarters are called. There probably isn't any real reason to do it in this order, but my methodical mind seems to want to work that way. Now, light the Goddess, then the God candles. Doing things in sequence helps to induce the frame of mind needed for successful ritual.

Sweeping the Circle

This is a way of cleansing the edge of the circle and should be done in a clockwise direction, starting in the north, sacred direction of witchcraft. The idea is to slowly work round, swishing the broom over the surface of the floor in a rhythmic fashion whilst visualising any psychic debris being dispersed. The sound of the broom is very soothing, and people often find it helps to trigger the right degree of relaxation to put them in the mood for the work that follows. Not all witches sweep the circle, but if you choose to do so, it adds to the measured and dancelike sequence of preparation in which each task can become a sacred act.

Centring

The purpose of this is to pull your awareness down from fixation on the head (the area Westerners usually regard as being their centre) and balance it between all the chakras prior to doing spiritual and psychic work. This sounds complicated but, in fact, is very simple and happens almost of its own accord once you are quiet and are breathing calmly. I had been automatically opening my chakras for years without giving it a second thought until I began to train for initiation, when I was earnestly "taught" how to do the very thing I was already doing of my own accord.

The chakras are centres where the layered sheaths of vital energy that surround our bodies are intensified. They correspond to places on the physical body and they can be seen as specific colours by the inner vision. When we are concentrating on daily pursuits in the outside world, they are smaller and less active than when we are engaged in creative, psychic, or ritual work; during this time they expand with glowing light and colour.

The lowest chakra, the *root chakra*, is red and is situated around the perineum, between the anus and vagina or testicles. It is our connection with the physical world and is a centre of vigour, strength, and health, and you will feel exhausted if it is blocked or depleted. The next chakra, the *sacral chakra*, is bright orange and located just below the navel. This is where we connect to our sexuality and to the ability to live in the material world without stress. Many Eastern religions see this as the place where spiritual and material meet, and in Tai Chi it is the point of equilibrium from which action proceeds. If you regularly shift your focus here during meditation, you will gradually become less affected by shock or trauma. Above this is the *solar plexus*, a radiant yellow centre where emotions are balanced. Anger or fear will tighten this chakra up and produce the well-known butterflies. Next is the *heart chakra*, which is emerald green and lies between the breasts. When we act from this centre we act selflessly. People who have been starved of love will have this centre constricted and may eventually have physical problems in this area if they don't find a way to heal it. In fact, stress or blockage in any chakra can lead to illness, though spiritual work and ritual will help the energies to flow freely again. The next chakra is the *throat chakra*; it is situated in the base of the throat, in the hollow above the collar bones, and is a deep aquamarine blue. It is the communication centre, and people who have difficulty expressing their feelings or who won't admit to anger may find themselves prone to sore throats. I suffered an annoying bout of laryngitis after finding myself in a situation where I was unable to speak out and stand up for myself—I was rendered literally speechless. Just between and above the eyebrows is the *brow chakra*, which is concerned with clairvoyance and visions and all visual work of a psychic and spiritual nature. It is glowing violet in colour. Sometimes people will experience headaches here when they are beginning to develop their psychic abilities. The last chakra, the *crown chakra*, extends from the crown of the head. It is radiant white and connects us to our spiritual source and to the universe as an interconnected whole.

Some systems see the colours and their placement slightly differently; for instance, indigo for the brow chakra and violet for the crown.

The fact of main importance is that we need to balance our energies between all the chakras. Although one or another may be predominant during particular activities, an overemphasis on any one centre can lead to disorientation or tiredness. This is particularly true if you get hooked on the top two chakras through overdoing visual or psychic work and ignore the more earthy centres or forget to ground yourself. It can be tempting to float around on a high, but ultimately you will feel disconnected.

The way to centre and open is to stand erect but relaxed with feet slightly apart. Begin to breathe calmly and deeply, gradually allowing the breath to reach lower into the lungs (many of us have tightened our bodies due to stress and breathe shallowly from the upper chest—a way of trying to keep the world from invading us). Let your awareness gradually sink lower and lower, like syrup drifting to the bottom of a glass of water. Now on the outward breath, let all worry and concern flow out of the nostrils. Let it go. See it leave you as a gray stream that will disperse harmlessly. On the inward breath, draw in prana, which is vital force and can be seen as golden white light, like sunlight. Let the whole sequence be calm and regular—you don't want to end up supercharged and bursting to run around. As you do this, begin to see your chakras slowly expanding, opening, and becoming brighter, starting with the root chakra and moving up in sequence. Don't worry if you can't feel anything definite; as long as you go through the visualisation, your energy centres will respond whether you are aware of it or not. When you feel ready, put incense on the charcoal in the censer and then proceed to the next stage of the ritual.

Consecrating Water and Salt

Water is seen by many religions as cleansing, and it is used by witches for this reason too. However, water does its work by absorbing any negativity in a space, thus purifying it. A bowl of water waiting on your altar will take up psychic impurities from the surrounding atmosphere, and these must be neutralised before the circle can be cleansed. For this reason, salt is added to the water. The salt itself, especially sea salt, is psychically inert and does not contain impurities, so it will keep the water pure when added to it.

The water must be "exorcised," which means that negative energies must be removed before the salt is added (don't worry too much about the subject of negativity; it mainly refers to the atmospheres and residues left by the ups and downs of ordinary daily living or, in slightly more dramatic circumstances, after an argument or illness or tension—we aren't talking poltergeists and hauntings here!). There are different ways to do this. One way is to hold the bowl in your hands and visualise it being flooded with white light that drives out and transmutes the unwanted residue. Another way to do this is to put the tip of your finger, wand, or athame in the water and direct a flow of cleansing light or energy into the bowl through this. Imagine the water being purified and charged. It really will feel and taste different afterward. If you want to, you can write an invocation to use while doing this. The one for initiatory Wicca is extremely beautiful, but the old-fashioned language used makes it sound quite dire and dramatic. Something along the lines of, "May this water be cleansed of all negativity that it might purify sacred space," is perfectly adequate. You will probably come up with something better than that.

Next, you need to bless the salt. It isn't necessary to cleanse salt, as it is already pure, but blessing it primes it for its work of "sterilising" the water and thanks the element of earth for its use. Direct energy into the salt the way you did with the water. Again, you can use an invocation, something like, "May this salt be blessed that it might protect the circle that I cast." If you want to use the Wiccan invocations, they can be found in books written by Alexandrian or Gardnerian witches. Similar ones can be found throughout pagan literature.

Now take three pinches of salt, add them to the water bowl, and gently mix them. If you use your athame for this, make sure you dry it well immediately after. The tip of mine got quite rusty at one time. Carry the bowl round the edge of the area, which will be your circle, starting at the north and moving clockwise. Sprinkle a ring of water as you go, visualising the saltwater cleansing this ring and beginning to form a barrier between you and the outside world. When you arrive back at the starting point, sprinkle yourself as well as anyone else present.

In Wicca, the water and salt are blessed and consecrated by a priestess, who also asperges the circle and all male coven members, using the sign relevant to the lowest degree attained among coven members present. Women are purified by a priest. It is common for Wiccan priestesses to be responsible for casting the circle as well.

Cleansing with the Elements

When we cleanse with water and salt we are also symbolically using the elements of earth and water. We also cleanse with fire and air, and this is done by carrying round the censer with its burning charcoal and smoky incense. Do exactly what you did with the water bowl, though now you are letting the smoke drift along the perimeter of the circle, imagining it cleansing and sealing your trail as you do so. It is not common practice, however, to use any invocations for the incense. Again, cleanse everyone present by passing the smoking censer up and over their bodies.

You are now ready to cast the circle.

Casting the Circle

The circle is cast by the power of the mind and by psychic or etheric energy drawn in through the aura and then directed out through one or more chakras. The implement used to direct this energy is simply a focusing tool, and it is perfectly possible to use the mind only. But certain tools help the mind to slip into gear, so to speak, and help it to focus and project power. The most commonly used tool for this is the athame or ritual knife, but you can use a wand, your finger, or a crystal instead if you prefer. One well-known English witch uses a lighted taper; this is spectacular to watch and produces a mega-charged circle.

Stand in the north of the circle. At this point I raise my athame in salute, then kiss the blade. This is a spontaneous gesture on my part, not something I would have thought would have been my style at all and a gesture I would find sentimental in any other context, but when I'm in the circle it seems right. I have seen other people do the same thing. You may or may not want to follow this practice of paying respect to the most sacred direction.

Point your athame (from now on I will say athame, but substitute pointing finger, wand, or whatever you choose) with your arm outstretched, ready to project power, and at the same time see yourself gathering etheric energy from the air around you (or the sky or the earth, whatever feels most natural to you). It may help to extend your other arm and imagine yourself drawing in the energy through it. It's important that you draw this substance from outside of yourself because otherwise you will drain your own supply and become tired. In your mind's eye, project this energy down your arm and out through the blade. The colour you perceive it to be will depend on which chakra you channel it through. Some people see it as golden solar plexus colour, some as white, some as violet, blue, or even a mix of these. "See" the light flowing from the blade to form a trail which, as you walk in a roughly circular shape round the room, will eventually seal itself when you reach your starting point. Some books tell you to stretch the ring of light to form a sphere or dome. I have tried that but find it takes a lot of time and concentration to do it properly. A ring of energy is just as effective and seems to grow of its own accord anyway, though seeing it projecting to form a thick barrier extending several feet from the tip of finger or blade helps. It also does-n't seem to make any difference if the circle isn't perfect. You can speak some words that relate to what you are doing if you like, starting when you reach the eastern quarter. Ask the circle to be powerful and secure, to be made sacred and to contain the energy of your working until you are ready to send it. Try something like, "Circle of power, be a boundary protecting me/us and the work I/we do. In the names of Goddess and God."

You have now completed the first steps that create sacred space between the worlds of everyday life and the spiritual realms. This is a place where time seems suspended (it is common practice to take off watches and hide the faces of clocks while in the circle) and the sounds and smells of out-side are filtered through, but faintly . . . even quite loud and sudden noises beyond the circle often go unnoticed by witches during a rite.

Calling in the Quarters

Each of the four directions in witchcraft relates to an ele-ment and all its qualities. Calling them into the circle cre-ates balance and stability. These elements—earth, fire, air, and water—are related to the actual elements of the same names but also have emotional and spiritual qualities akin to the medieval humours and the suits of tarot. Some people think of them as beings on another level of existence that is linked to ours, others as mighty Kings, and still others as natural forces that can be channelled and focused for the duration of the rite. How you perceive the elements is very much a personal matter and no two people will have exactly the same understanding of them. What is certain is that they are part of religious practice all over the world, from Tibetan Buddhism to the Native American Medicine Wheel; even Islam and Christianity honour the directions in the way they orientate their places of worship. I will describe them in the order in which you will encounter them while casting a circle.

The first of these elements, and the least solid or visible, is air. Its direction is east, its time of year spring, and its time of day dawn; its creatures are birds and its colour yellow or blue, according to the tradition you follow. It is a masculine element. Its magical tools are the athame and sword. Air is detached and rational. It rules the intellect, the thought processes, the wind, and breezes. It also rules the breath, which, in many spiritual traditions, is the vehicle of creation.

The second element is fire, also masculine, which belongs to the south, to midday, to summer. Fire is dramatic, passionate, creative but childlike. Its colour is red and its creatures are salamanders, dragons, lions, and horses. Its magical tool is the wand or stave. For many religions, fire represents the spirit, and this is echoed by the use of candles or a sanctuary flame.

The third element is water and its direction is west, its time sunset, and its season autumn. It is feminine. Water is rain, mist, rivers, streams, pools, waterfalls, and the restless, ever-moving sea . . . all metaphors for different emotional states. It is intuitive, emotional, elusive, persistent, compassionate, and psychic. The animals for water are whales, dolphins, fishes, and other water creatures; its colour is blue. Its magical tools are the chalice and the cauldron.

The fourth element is earth; it is feminine and its direction is north. Earth is green, brown, or yellow, according to different sources. It represents rocks, soil, crystals, mountains, caves and standing stones, and all green and growing things. Its magical tool is the pentacle. Earth is stolid, dependable, phlegmatic, patient, fruitful, and enduring. Its animals are the bear, cattle, and all small tunnelling creatures like moles. This is the most sacred direction in witchcraft and paganism and connects us to our Mother, the Great Goddess of old.

There is a fifth element called ether. It belongs to the centre of the circle and the topmost point of the pentagram and stands for spirit. Its colours are white and violet.

The eastern quarter is summoned first. Walk clockwise to that area of the circle and stand in front of the eastern point candle. There are three ways to begin the summoning of the eastern quarter. The first is very simple: you visualise a strong yellow light bathing that part of the circle. The second way is to inscribe a yellow pentagram in the air with your athame or just your mind. You would start at the top left and move down, as shown in the diagram.

INVOKING PENTAGRAM

The third way for each element, which is done in Wicca, is to draw a pentagram of the appropriate colour moving in the direction appropriate to the element you are summoning.

Next, conjure up images and qualities that are associated with the air element. Some people like to see the animals associated with each of the quarters, such as an eagle or hawk for air. I see myself on a windy mountaintop at dawn—the air is full of springtime freshness and there are yellow streaks of cloud in the sky. When you have been working in a particular place for some time, casting several circles over a period of weeks, the quarters will come in positively and quickly without much input from you, but initially you need to work hard on building up your visualisation. Often, too, one or another element will seem stronger than the others at certain times. Frequently, the candle in that quarter will spark or flare or flicker more than usual, even though there is no draught, or else there will be a strong and almost tangible aura relating to the qualities of the element in question. This sometimes happens at the festivals or with the full moon, when the element is strengthened by astrological association.

At this point, it is normal to speak to the element you are summoning. Different branches of paganism have different invocations, but all refer in some way to the quarter being invoked. This invocation can be spontaneous, written beforehand, or taken from traditional sources. The traditional ones run something like this: "Ye Mighty Ones of the East," or "Lords of the East," and proceed with declarations of summoning or inviting the spirits of air, fire, water, or earth to come into the circle, to guard and empower the work done in it. A spontaneous one might go like this: "Rushing wind, dawn freshness, springtime, be with us now. Bring us your qualities of detachment and rationalisation. Help us to think clearly in the work we do. Empower and protect our circle." The main thing is that you are asking that element to be present and to lend its qualities to your ritual whilst also stabilising and protecting the circle. Whatever you say must reflect that. One of my students once planned a ritual where we acted out the qualities of each element to summon them and didn't use words at all, but nonetheless, we were thinking of their protective and empowering attributes. When you have invoked air, bid its elemental powers "Hail and welcome." When that is done, you are ready to move on to fire.

Repeat the actions for calling in the elements for each quarter in turn, visualising their qualities, colour, and so on, moving from fire and south to water and west and finally earth and north. With fire, try visualising reds and oranges, flames, the high midday summer sun; with water, the twilit seashore and blue-green waves where whales or dolphins play; with earth, standing stones or mountains, caves, or rich soil and growing plants. These are only suggestions and you will evolve your own way of working.

Raising Energy

The circle is now cast and you can move on to the next stage of the ritual, which concerns the raising of energy. Some people like to call the Goddess and God first, but I found that it works best for me to call them after power has been raised because the energy serves as a vehicle for inner vision and so they come in more strongly and dramatically. The actual methods of raising power have been covered in the chapter on magical tools.

Invoking Goddess or God

Although both deities are usually called into the circle (for those of us who work with both), sometimes a ritual is centred around only one of them, but the pattern of invocation is the same.

The Goddess and God can be invoked into the circle generally, to be felt by everyone there, or they can be channelled through individuals. In Wicca it is quite common for a man to call down the qualities of the Goddess through a woman present and for a woman to invoke the God through a man (though men can invoke the God and women the Goddess). This is done by calling on the particular deity in question and asking them to enter the intended vessel, and is the basis of the well-known "Drawing Down the Moon." What happens is a blend of overshadowing that person's personality and calling out qualities from within them that match, or indeed are, the energy of Goddess or God. This sounds sinister when described, but the person involved is not entranced or possessed and remains aware at all times, though they may feel remote or strange and may find themselves speaking profoundly and spontaneously in a voice that is different from their normal voice.

It is more common for the deity to be invoked into the circle generally; if this is done, then everybody there is likely to be aware of that presence, though the perceptions of each group member will probably vary. The way to do this is to stand with the back to the altar and speak words of welcome such as: "Lady of the full moon, Great Mother, bring us beauty and strength, joy and compassion. Be with us now." You can write something first, use something from a book, or be spontaneous. Do the same to invoke the God, tailoring the invocation to his qualities. If you want to call in a particular deity, learn about them first. Also, be careful who you call on . . . do you really want Loki if you are doing a ritual for peace and tranquillity, or Pan if you are working on an alcohol problem? When the Goddess or God are present you can ask them to bless and empower your working.

Remember that in one sense you are not calling in a presence from outside alone but from within yourself and everyone with you as well. The universe is a seamless whole and everything within it is not only linked but, on one level, is part of everything else; in sacred space we become more aware of that. Trust your responses and be open to whatever experiences happen to you. Goddess and God are universal energies that are nonetheless open to individual interpretation. The ways they have been depicted over the ages are symbolic representations that have been fashioned by the cultures who first gave them names or assigned particular qualities to them. We will experience Isis in a very different way than that of the ancient Egyptians, who themselves gave her different attributes as time went on. But even so, the energies that come into the circle have a reality that will become more prominent as you practice over the months.

If you don't think you are experiencing Goddess and God to begin with, don't worry. Often, profound experiences take place deep within us and we only become aware of them later when they surface as dreams or as enhanced perceptions. Be patient.

Working

You don't have to do magic during every ritual. You don't have to do it all if you don't want to. Some witches and Wiccans never do spells and instead use the circle for healing or communing with the gods. If you do decide to include magic in your ritual, it often works best to do it before anything like meditation or scrying. That way you can make use of the energy you have raised to prime your spell. Then you can go ahead and concentrate on any meditation, divinatory work, or pathworking that you want to do.

Sometimes it is good to work on the festivals, as they can give an extra boost to spells. Other times it feels right to use these times for communion and celebration alone. What you do is up to you and there is no right or wrong way, no one way that will suit everybody. The moon's phases can also be used for healing, self-realisation, or understanding aspects of the Goddess or God, as well as for magical work.

Spells are covered in the section on magic, but I will say a few additional words here. First, don't overload the ritual. It is difficult to keep the same firmness of purpose for more than three goals per person. Magic works best for those desires that are keenly felt. If you are halfhearted about it or spread yourself too thin, you won't be able to put the same amount of energy into your working and it won't be as potent. For the same reason, keep things simple. Often, planting seeds in a bowl to represent wishes that you want to grow into reality is effective as is and needs no further embellishment. Candle spells are equally simple and effective. Be inventive as well. If you want to lose weight, carve *healthy weight loss* on a black candle when the moon is waning and let it burn down between then and the new moon; every time you light it and put it out, *see* yourself getting slimmer and healthier. Use symbolic equivalents if you like: sugar to bring sweetness into your life; salt or earth to represent stability. A simple smiley face drawn on a piece of paper and left under an orange candle as it burns will leave you feeling cheerful and positive for days.

Sometimes, after you have done your magical work, the atmosphere in the circle is so lovely that you don't want to bring the ritual to an end, and this is a prime time to meditate. You can start by sitting and enjoying the energy around you. Gradually relax and deepen your breathing as you did when centring before the circle was cast. Let your eyes close but don't shut them tightly . . . keep everything relaxed and calm while absorbing the spiritual ambience. You may find that you are going into a light trance in which visions or insights come to you. Or you may want to gain insights about a particular aspect of witchcraft, like one of the elements, for instance. Bring that into your mind and concentrate on it, allowing your intuition to open up meanings for you.

Equally, at this point in the rite, you may simply want to sit back, relax, and enjoy the flowers, incense, and candlelight.

Some individuals and groups use drugs to enhance their perceptions and encourage vision. I prefer not to use drugs or alcohol in the circle; for me they are disorientating and leave me with a clogged auric residue. Some people find them helpful, especially in a shamanic context. What you do is your choice and your right (morally if not legally), but if you do use drugs, be sensible and don't experiment with unknown fungi or herbs.

Sooner or later you will sense that it is time to conclude whatever work you are doing. It may be a feeling that the ritual is drawing to a close, or you may find yourself thinking of mundane concerns or wondering what the time is. It is now time to bless the food and drink.

Feasting

I use this term loosely, since your "feast" may consist of as little as a chalice of juice and a biscuit.

This part of the rite serves two ends. First, it grounds those present, since eating and drinking closes the chakras and returns one to a normal, everyday state. This is extremely important; I have attended workshops where people have been sent out without being fully grounded and have been unable to function properly for a while (a state that could be extremely dangerous if you have to negotiate busy streets to get home). You will know this applies to you if you feel vague or spacey and your eyes look glassy. The second function is to give thanks for the rewards of the ritual while communing with others present. If you are on your own, this is a time to relax and come back down to earth.

The ritual feast is often called *Cakes and Wine*, but what you eat and drink is up to you. Our group seldom has a huge feast. When I work on my own, I often just grab some fruit and juice. I have been known to have cola in my chalice for want of anything more appropriate . . . not the most apt of libations perhaps, but it does the job! The coven I was initiated into often had a huge cooked meal; the members came from long distances to work together and seldom saw each other between rituals so their meetings were important social occasions to them as well as spiritual events.

In the chalice you could have juice, wine, or spring water. Sensitivity and tact are needed if some participants are known to have an alcohol problem. Small groups will be aware of any problems and should provide an alternative. In Britain, there is a widespread wine and real ale bias among pagans with an assumption that alcohol and paganism are synonymous, and this can cause stress for nondrinkers. I feel there is a need to address this problem, particularly in large public group rituals, where ideally wine should either be excluded from the group chalice or else a second chalice with a nonalcoholic alternative sent round.

Food can be as simple or as decorative as you want. We sometimes bake biscuits in the form of a crescent moon; these are called moon cakes and are usually made with butter and dusted with icing sugar (powdered sugar), though healthier recipes can be used instead! At the eight festivals, I sometimes use a cutter in the shape of a deer. Other alternatives are fruit or cake. For convenience, many people (my group included) sometimes purchase cakes or biscuits from a bakery.

The chalice and its contents are blessed before being passed in a clockwise direction round any participants. You can raise it and say some words, either spontaneous or planned. These words involve dedicating the contents of the chalice to the Goddess or God and asking for it to spiritually empower or uplift those who consume it. At full moon rites I sometimes visualise the energy of the moon streaming into the chalice and transmuting the contents. Another way to do this is to put the point of wand or athame in the liquid and let it focus your blessing. Plunging the athame into the chalice at this point in the ritual can serve the dual purpose of symbolising the male and female energies, Goddess and God, united. This is a sacred act, the sexual symbolism of which is obvious, and forms an important part of Wiccan ritual. To me, it is the core of meaning within the whole tradition, and, as such, is deeply moving and beautiful.

The chalice is now passed clockwise round the circle. It is common for people to say "Blessed Be" as they give and receive the chalice, and this is taken from the five-fold kiss of initiatory Wicca. There is something very special and bonding about sharing the chalice in this way, even among strangers who have come together for a public rite.

Similarly, the food is blessed and asked to ground and sustain those present, then is passed round clockwise for people to take their share.

We now come to the concluding part of the ritual.

Opening the Circle

After a ritual, it is important to remove the energies that were used to build sacred space. Left to gradually disperse, they will disorientate and possibly disrupt the normal balance of a living space.

First, thank the Goddess or God for their presence and for any strength or help they have given and respectfully bid them farewell.

Now you are ready to thank and dismiss the quarters. Walk to the east. If you have drawn an invoking pentagram, draw one going the opposite way; that is, start at the point that was the conclusion of the previous pentagram, as shown on the following page.

BANISHING PENTAGRAM

See the pentagram being taken up, or vanishing, as you do this. If you conjured the colour yellow alone, see this disappearing. Imagine the qualities of air fading back and that part of the room returning to its everyday state. Speak to the elemental powers of air, thank them for their presence and help, and bid them "Hail and Farewell." Then snuff the eastern candle. Walk round to each of the quarters in turn and repeat the process. Finally, snuff the altar candles.

You will perceive that the room is cooler and feels more "open." The outside world will seem to rush in and sounds will become more noticeable. It is now time to clear everything away and wash out the chalice and water bowl. At this point, some groups will kiss each other and say "Merry meet and merry part and merry meet again" to convey that the companionship of the circle is something that continues into daily life and will come into focus again at the next ritual.

Some people like to save a little of the contents of the chalice and some food to sprinkle on the ground in offering to the gods and the ancestors after the rite is ended. Others may pour the salted water on the earth outside, but this should be done with care, as salt water will pollute the soil and kill plants.

Although the etheric energy that constructed the circle has now been dispersed, an uplifting aura will often remain for several days after a ritual.

The regular practice of ritual is something that strengthens, centres, and empowers us, putting us in touch with each other, with nature, and with the meaning behind our spiritual practice. Our joy and understanding will increase and we will become more balanced individuals, able to cope with whatever life throws at us. Furthermore, we will learn that spirituality does not have to be a serious matter (though it can be), and that it's okay to joke and laugh in the circle. We don't have to conduct ourselves in a solemn manner; if we forget to light the charcoal block for incense, or trip over each others' feet, it is not the end of the world. If we forget our spell candle till after the circle is cast, that doesn't matter either . . . it's all right to devise another spell instead. Witchcraft is a living and growing tradition, and part of its strength lies in the creative and inventive input of its practitioners.

Some invocations and ritual plans can be used over and over again, and they will gain beauty and power with every repeat. Others can and should be added to or adapted. Some rites can be totally spontaneous, or meticulously planned. If you cast the circle and discover that your carefully written words don't fit the current energies, you can change them to follow the flow of the moment.

If you always work alone, you will perform all parts of the ritual yourself. If you work as part of a group, one person can be assigned the role of high priestess and one of high priest; group members can alternate the roles, taking it in turns, or everyone can share the different tasks involved. If everyone takes a turn at invoking a particular quarter, and if people move from one element to another over the course of several rituals, then each person gets a chance to experience the elements in turn and to understand and strengthen any elemental weaknesses within themselves. Similarly, a great deal of growth and love will become apparent between group members who take it in turns to cleanse and cast the circle and share any other parts of the rite.

Finally, once the circle is cast, ideally nobody should leave. Walking through the edge of the circle can sometimes disperse the protective barrier it forms. If it becomes necessary to leave, cut an entranceway by moving finger or athame from ground upward, then over and down to form an "outline" large enough to step through. When you come back through, seal the gap by going over it again in a clockwise direction and visualising it closing.

CHAPTER THIRTEEN

Lammas

Apples are ripening and the green holly berries are flushed with bronze. Bees meander from sunflowers to late-blooming roses, drugged with heat; and garden tigers, beautiful moths with wings striped orange and midnight blue, settle among mint and lemon balm or spread their wings against the brickwork at the back of the house. Japanese anemones unfurl their delicate petals by the front gate where a white clematis lifts exotic, luminous faces to the moon each night. Toads venture down the path in the long evenings, forsaking the cool leaf mould at the bottom of the garden as they search for insects. The lilacs have dried to seeds, and rich brown conkers (the fruit of the horse chestnut) hide in their spiky cases where, before, the candles of spring burned.

The corn is ripe now, heavy and dry and deep gold, and some fields have already been cut. The long, still days are overshadowed by forthcoming sacrifice and the Goddess has begun to surrender the harvest. Soon she will lose her lover, the fruit of her womb. My heart is pierced with sadness for her and I think of Mary standing at the foot of the cross—for Jesus was also a dying and resurrecting god and Christianity tells an age-old tale in a new way.

I think also of the plenty that surrounds us all in the Western world, where we have the luxury of pursuing personal goals over and above the need to feed our bodies. In the Third World, people are not so fortunate. Their priority is survival from day to day; life and death are inextricably linked with the grain, and feeding their children now may mean there can be no harvest next year; yet if the corn is planted, the rains that nourish the seed may not come anyway. May the children of the world cease to hunger, in both body and spirit, and may everyone have enough for their needs . . . whatever they may be.

On the first day of August we all gather in Moira's garden. Her table is laden with bread of different kinds, for this is the first harvest, the grain harvest, and Lammas takes its name from the Saxon word for half loaf, the sacred bread made from the earliest cut corn.

That evening, on a hillside overlooking the corn fields, when the moon has risen huge and round and red-streaked gold above the horizon, we four meet to pay homage to the King. Our circle is open to the night, for the land and the starry dome of the sky will be our sacred space. No candles light our actions. The moonlight floods the countryside and casts strange shadows. It is almost as bright as day as we link hands and dance together silently. We don't want to attract others who may disturb our rite, so we keep everything quiet and low-key.

The Lady and her Lord are all around us, in every breath we draw, in the breeze that briefly ruffles the warm air. The earth gives off their essence in the scents of thyme and dry soil, and we hear their voices when some night creature cries out and an owl hoots far away across the valley.

Arms raised, Robin intones softly, "You who were the Great Mother of old, we honour your sacrifice. We give thanks for our personal harvest, and we offer up our own sacrifice, for we must relinquish all that has failed in our lives even though we know that letting go of cherished dreams is hard."

One by one, we voice the things we have gained since Yule and the things that we need to put behind us, everything from deeply personal emotional issues to financial ones, and, as ever, the glowing patterning of our spiritual ups and downs. Tears blur my eyes briefly as I admit to one particularly longed-for goal that I now realise will never come into being. I feel my heart wrench with pity as the Goddess speaks in me, telling me how she must nourish and birth the Lord of her life year after year only to lose him as the Wheel turns to harvest again. How trivial is the little lack in my well-fed existence when set against the loss of life across the planet as war and hunger take their toll?

I raise the chalice of crimson grape juice in silent tribute to the Lord, whose blood this represents. I spill some on the ground, splattering the ears of corn we have collected, then we drink in turn. One of us has a history of alcohol abuse and must be safeguarded, so we do not use wine. From now until Yule we will lose the God from the world and must seek him in the dark reaches of our own subconscious minds—the Underworld to where he withdraws to watch over the gates of death.

When all is done and our ritual ended, we drift down the hillside and wander into fields where the wheat has been felled. Our feet brush through stubble, startling those small creatures who have escaped the blades of the combine harvester and now seek refuge under the spilled straw. The moon has risen higher and pours its radiance over our blanched faces. We move silently, *minds connected, as we share in the emotional aftermath of the rite. Although we are surrounded by warmth and abundance, we can feel the threat of colder, darker times. The Goddess is withdrawing her benevolence, becoming the Cailleagh of Celtic times, the Hag. Yet, as in the stories where the ugly crone becomes the radiant girl, so the miracle of renewal will make a maiden of her once more at spring. Within her shrivelling womb the new God is already forming. Life in death, death in life, nature shows us the meaning behind those things that cause us pain.*

Lammas, or Lughnasahd, is a cross-quarter fire festival and is celebrated on the evening of July 31 and on August 1, 2, and 3. The sun is in Leo.

Lammas is the first harvest, the time when we reap the rewards of the seeds sown in this year's cycle, both literally in terms of the corn and wheat that the farmers have planted and that will feed us when they reach our shops as flour and bread, and metaphorically in the form of the goals we have worked on since we lit our wish candles at Imbolc. But in the midst of all this abundance is death. The God is cut down in the fields to go into the earth, to fulfill the sacrifice that leads to renewal. In our own lives we reap the harvest of our prior intentions, but must let go of much that has had its season so that there is room for new growth.

In Celtic times, when this was the feast of Lugh and the festival of first fruits, celebrations would probably have gone on for the whole of August. Lugh was a Celtic fire god, a sacrificial god who was cut down with the harvest and who, in later times, became John Barleycorn. The God can also be seen as the mature Lord married to the Goddess as the land, and responsible for the survival and well-being of his people. Ancient sacrificed kings were a representative of the God, and the old tradition of August or Lughnasahd weddings reflects both the offering up of the God and the marriage to the land.

This festival also celebrates the more ancient theme of the Goddess as Corn Mother, she who gives birth to the harvest. But the forces of growth that began to emerge at Imbolc must now return into the earth to rest and sustain the soil before the next growth cycle. This is symbolised by the Corn Mother going into the burial mounds to become the Cailleagh, the Winter Hag, to await her emergence as the Corn Bride at Imbolc. A Corn Mother can be made now, then dressed in white as the Corn Bride when Imbolc comes. In the old farming communities, she would have been fashioned from the last sheaf of corn to be cut during harvest.

Our own energies begin to gear down now, too, ready for the inward turn at the Equinox and the descent to the depths at Samhain. We have to make sacrifices also, exchanging our failures and outgrown phases in exchange for reaping the harvest of our spring and summer endeavours.

Food is in abundance and can be symbolised on the altar by wheat and corn, fruit and bread. This is the only time when pagans symbolically drink the blood of the God in the form of red wine or juice, and this is the meaning behind the later Christian version of holy communion.

CHAPTER FOURTEEN

Magic

Tarot, astrology, meditation, healing, and pathworking are all part of magical work. However, what most people mean by magic is spell crafting.

When I first began to consciously practice witchcraft, I was wary of using magic. I thought that I would be taking something I wasn't entitled to . . . maybe opening myself up to some kind of harm or damage (I wasn't sure what). I even thought that I might be usurping power that was meant for some authority other than myself. This vague and slightly superstitious attitude toward magic is common in our culture, which, though no longer outwardly Christian, has been partly shaped by repressive Judeo-Christian values for nearly two millennia (I am not criticising all Christians here, but only those who, throughout history, have been intolerant of other spiritual paths. It may shock you to know that there are fundamentalists in paganism also). In training groups for new pagans, most often almost everyone present is comfortable with being pagan, eager to explore ritual, the elements, meditation, and so on, but most are ambivalent about magic.

The fact is that all of us are shaping our reality from moment to moment all our lives. The way we think, the way we react and behave sets forces in motion, triggers energies that shape our circumstances and impact on the lives of others. It might be comforting to think it is all fate and beyond our control, but the reality is that we and everything else in the universe are linked and whatever we choose to do (or not do) will yield results. This is inevitable and unavoidable and is the basis of karma. Therefore, it is ultimately more rewarding *and* more responsible to take control of our own destinies and form our lives in a mature and creative fashion, as far as we are able. The repercussions of whatever we do will come back to us in some form, so why not willingly take up that responsibility and make sure that the harvest we reap is as beneficial to ourselves and our environment as we are able to make it. I had always been able to get what I needed by being so determined that I wouldn't accept the possibility of defeat (though I have *never* been prepared to trample anyone else in the process). The moment I acknowledged this I was able to accept that magic is only immoral when practised with an irresponsible disregard for the rights of others and the well-being of the earth we live on.

Life is energy. Magic is energy shaped by the mind toward a specified purpose. As we think, so do we live. People who are optimistic often seem to enjoy success and contentment; those who are pessimistic find life a struggle and are weighed down by unfortunate events and missed opportunities. Some circumstances are unavoidable, and then we can only work to alleviate the worst of the results and hope the process will bring us growth. However, many situations can be eased or modified if we are determined and if we believe in our own ability to change things.

Many religions advocate prayer, and this is another way of shaping energy and directing it toward a goal, and, if practised with belief, will very often bring about the desired result. In witchcraft we do not ask a higher authority to do this work for us—though we may call on the power of Goddess and God or the elemental guardians of the circle to give our spells a boost—instead we are our own authority and take full responsibility for our actions and their results. We also set certain safeguards around ourselves. We always work with the proviso that what we do is without violating the free will of someone else and that we do not harm ourselves or others in the pursuit of our goals. It is perfectly acceptable to do magic to open up circumstances so that you can find a better paying job—it is *not* okay to do a spell to steal another person's job, no matter how suitable you think it would be for you. Nor must you ever, *ever* use magic to manipulate somebody and try to bend their will to yours, and this includes people you would like as lovers or even friends. No good could ever come of it. It is unlikely you can emotionally enslave someone like this, and even if you could, what would be the point of holding them to you when they don't truly care about you in return? The best you can hope for is that they will be temporarily fascinated by you . . . when the glamour wears off you will probably be left feeling rejected and lonelier than before. It isn't worth it.

Whatever magic you practice will work in some way; if it can't bring about exactly what you have asked for, it will bring the nearest equivalent; the energy, once raised and shaped, has to go somewhere. Doing magic will bring changes into your life, so you had better be prepared to work with the results. For this reason it is sensible to think very carefully about what you want and to allow flexible leeway. That house you have set your heart on may bring a whole new life direction that you will later regret. It is better to work for that particular house *if* it is right for you, or to ask to find the house that is the right one, whether it is the one you fancy living in or another that you may not have seen yet but that may be more suitable. Also be prepared for the fact that magic will sometimes fail to manifest the desired results because you yourself have blocked it. No matter how eagerly we may embrace change on a conscious level, all of us have subconscious blocks and fears that may impede our progress from time to time and that need to be gradually and patiently resolved before we can move forward. In fact, on a deep level, magic is more about resolving emotional and psychological issues than about changing outer circumstances . . . though if we change ourselves, our outer lives will inevitably change as well. Interacting with life and working through situations bring spiritual growth. If we apply the wise use of magic to our life's path, we are working in harmony with the needs of our deep selves, the part of us that desires our highest good.

With all forms of magic, it can really help to make a kind of mental sidestep so that you tell yourself that the thing you want is already in your life, or that it cannot fail to come to you.

In performing magic, we need to align ourselves with the tides of moon, sun, and the seasons. The waxing moon brings increase, the full moon realisation and fulfillment, and the waning moon brings decrease or the ebbing away of the old. Yule to Oestara is a preparation and seeding time,

Beltane to Lammas is concerned with the cultivation and harvest of our purposes, and the Autumn Equinox to Samhain and Yule again is a time to work through what has already been attained and to sort and process what needs to be resolved or discarded when the next solar cycle begins (the festivals themselves are potent times on which to work magically and spiritually). Even the days of the week can be included, so that Saturday is for constriction, consolidation, and building; Sunday is for enjoyment, creativity, and gain; Monday is for psychic or emotional matters or for dealing with family; Tuesday is for competition and standing up for yourself; Wednesday is about commerce and communication; Thursday involves spirituality, education, and travel; and Friday relates to love, friendship, and socialising. A spell for prosperity will probably work on any day of the week and time of the year as long as it is done from new to full moon, but doing the same spell on a Sunday and during the waxing half of the year will give it extra help. Astrological transits are also part of the picture, and it is best to go with them as far as possible. When you have Saturn moving through your fourth house, which means home and family, it might be better to concentrate on consolidating and securing your existing home rather than trying to move somewhere else; a Jupiter transit might be a good time to work on prosperity, to travel, or for spiritual and religious study, and so on.

A successful spell will bring you opportunities. If you need money, you will not find it showering through your mailbox and you are not likely to win the lottery (though it isn't impossible!), but you will find that sooner or later the chance comes along to change to a better paying job, or to exchange a skill for monetary payment. Whatever you take from life must be paid for—there is nothing sinister about this, it is a simple matter of energy exchange. When I'm hard up and do a money spell, I often find I have an increase in clients wanting tarot readings or astrological charts. This is a particularly rewarding way of getting what I want because I am helping others at the same time. The gardening you do in exchange for pay is also helping someone who probably doesn't have the time or perhaps the physical health to do it for themselves. If you do a stint of babysitting, you are giving someone a chance to earn money themselves or to have a much-needed break. If you state, during your spell working, that you want the highest good for everyone concerned, then your results will always benefit anyone who is involved.

Magic is shaped by our intentions and works best when we have such need that our whole concentration is focused on a particular result. This is why it is difficult to make magic work on someone else's behalf, unless they are in the circle with you and you are working mutually for each others' needs. No matter how altruistic your outlook or intentions, unless the person on whose behalf you are working is close to you, it will be difficult to summon the necessary motivation. Aside from this, you should not be made responsible for another's life in this way. It would be better to persuade them to do the spell with you under your guidance. It goes without saying that it is a gross infringement of someone else's free will to work magic for them without their permission or knowledge—and, with a few exceptions, this applies to healing as well. We do not have the right to judge another's circumstances and needs, and we may do untold damage if we meddle. I have had healing directed at me by a well-meaning friend who was taken aback when I told her that I was becoming spaced-out and disorientated by her efforts. Another time I had my sleep disturbed at five o'clock every morning, eventually discovering that someone

I knew was getting up and praying for me then. What made it worse was that the situation in my life that had drawn such fervent interference was something I was tackling in my own way—and this was bringing me growth and satisfaction. This is a dodgy area, so tread carefully and when in doubt, *don't*.

Some spells will give quick results but won't last, whereas the effects of others will take longer to manifest but will be more enduring. When I first started doing magic, I couldn't understand why, while I got what I wanted almost straight away, the results didn't endure and I would have to reinforce the working at a later date. I was mostly using candle magic and was letting the candle burn out overnight. When I began to train with someone else, I was told to light the candle every day or night for an extended period (any time from a week to a month), and this practice secured much more lasting results. Of course, sometimes you will want things to work quickly, as in when you want a short burst of confidence to get you through an imminent job interview, or when an emergency arises that cannot wait on a more protracted working.

Whatever you choose to do, magic is only a prop; the real working is done with your mind. But using an object during a spell gives you a focus for your willpower and concentration and makes you feel you are doing something positive. Within the circle, the rational mind takes a back seat to the imaginative self, which is happiest when given simplistic tasks to perform. Using a green candle of itself won't bring you prosperity, but focusing on the elemental properties of the colour will help you to concentrate your intent. Ideally, you should back this up with a relevant, simple rhyme, but I have never been particularly good at this and so stick to a short proclamation instead.

There are many different ways to perform magic, and I will deal with some of the better known methods in turn.

Candle Magic

Candle magic is simple, satisfying, and gentle. There are slightly different ways to go about it so I will describe the way I have found works best for me. You can adapt it to suit yourself. You don't have to work within a circle, but a cast circle helps to concentrate the power contained within. You can also raise energy, which will infuse the spell with power.

Always use fresh candles. If you use a candle that has been burned for another purpose, you will be mixing vibrations together and may muddle or negate your spell. Have a holder ready. Cleanse the candle through the elements. Now hold it in your hands and put it to your third eye while you visualise the conditions you want it to bring into your life. Take your time over this and keep up a steady concentration of energy whilst seeing the candle "saturated" with the thoughts you are forming.

When you feel ready, light the candle from a taper, a match, or one of the altar candles whilst saying words such as, "I light this candle to bring . . . (intent). To the free will of all and the highest good of all concerned. In the name of the Goddess and God. So mote it be. Blessed be." *So mote it be* means "so must" or "so shall" it be (which you are at liberty to say instead if you want) and is a widely used affirmation in pagan circles. Let the candle burn for a while but put it out when you open the circle. Put it in a fireproof container such as a cauldron, or in some other safe place. Light it on subsequent evenings or nights for a specified length of time; I usually burn a little bit each day for the rest of that moon's cycle or until the moon returns to the same phase. When you relight the candle, briefly restate your purpose and when you put it out, visualise how your life will be when the goal is realised. Keep this up till the candle has burned right down, even if what you want happens before the candle is used up. Often your result will begin to manifest quite soon; continuing with the ritual of lighting and putting out the candle will fix the spell so that it sticks.

Always snuff or pinch out candles. I was taught that blowing them out is the equivalent of using the life force to annihilate something, because the breath is a vehicle for prana or vitality.

The following are some colour correspondences for candle magic. Other sources will give slightly different variations and it is wise to read from as many books as possible, then decide for yourself what to use.

Red: Health, vitality, purpose, passion, courage.

Orange: Confidence or ambition, especially relating to career or dealing with the public. Use with care! I once burned an orange candle overnight to give me the confidence to speak out in a group situation the next day. The trouble was I couldn't shut up. My mouth seemed to run away with me; I could hear myself speaking out in a very upfront and pushy manner but couldn't seem to stop. Maybe the problem was that I'm already quite confident and didn't need additional help.

Yellow: Mental work, the intellect, study.

Green: Growth, fertility, healing, and prosperity. I sometimes use a spring green for new moon spells when I want a condition to grow throughout the current moon's phase. Deeper green is more earthing and brings solid, lasting results.

Blue: Tranquillity, harmony, meditation, patience, peace, detachment, spirituality.

Purple: Spiritual learning, higher education, religion, writing, travel.

Pink: Dark pink for sexual passion and love. Light pink for love, harmony, and friendship.

Gold: Money specifically, as opposed to prosperity in general. The sun.

Silver: The moon, purity.

White: Purity, peace, protection, spirituality. If you don't have other colours or don't want to use them, white can be used for almost any spell.

Black: Banishing or eliminating the unwanted from your life. Weight loss. Letting go.

Some essential oils can be used in conjunction with candles to enhance their effectiveness. Rub the candle from tip to centre and then from base to centre before priming with your intent.

Patchouli: Prosperity, male fertility, earth energy.

Cinnamon: Prosperity, energy.

Lavender: Purification, protection, calmness, and healing.

Sandalwood: Protection, meditation.

Rose: Love, friendship, harmony, and well-being.

Cord Magic

Take a cord of the appropriate colour for your purpose (refer to the candle correspondences or the colours mentioned under cords in the chapter on magical tools). Consecrate it through the elements in turn, then hold it till you have empowered it with your intent. Next, tie a secure knot in the centre of the cord, concentrating on the reason for the spell as you do so. When this is done, say, "I've knotted one, the spell's begun." Go now to one end of the cord and say, "I've knotted two, it cometh true." Remember to affirm your intention mentally with each knot. Work across the cord following the diagram below.

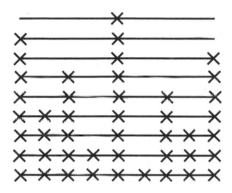

CORD MAGIC

The words for the remaining sequence of knots are: "I've tied three, so will it be; I've tied four, its strength is more; I've tied five, it comes alive; I've tied six, the spell to fix; I've tied seven, the stars of heaven; I've tied eight, and seal its fate; I've tied nine, and make it mine." There are minor variations on these words, but this is the basis of traditional cord magic.

When you have done your cord spell you can put it in a special box on your shrine, wear it, or bury it. Some authorities suggest untying the knots once the spell has worked. Sometimes, however, the spell is ongoing and then I find it best to leave the cord alone and forget about it.

Directed Power

There are several ways of doing this, and first you must raise energy by clapping, dancing, chanting, drumming, and the like. The energy can then be shaped and directed into an object such as a candle or a bowl of seeds, or spun and sent onto the astral level to grow from seeds of intention into material reality—for this is the place where ideas are shaped into the things we experience in our everyday lives.

The energy within the circle is electric and yet fluid and malleable. Everybody sees it differently, but most people agree that it is like bright light. Its coloration depends on the predominant element at the time it is raised, but it is often a glowing, brilliant white, as opposed to energy focused through an athame when casting the circle, which will usually be white, blue, violet, or golden depending on which chakra the person directing it draws it through.

Power sent onto the astral is formed into a sphere or cone by a group visualising themselves pushing it with their linked hands, or just their minds . . . it is quite difficult to do this on your own. As it spins and picks up speed, everybody "sees" their spell or intention being woven into it. When the cone or sphere is spinning really fast, there comes a point when one or more of a group will feel the climax of power approaching and will give the signal to release the power (usually by breaking the link or by calling "Now!"). Discharging energy like this will leave you feeling exhilarated but tired and you will need to eat and drink soon after to replenish yourself.

Spells of increase require that you spin energy clockwise, while banishing spells need a counterclockwise direction. This is because in the northern hemisphere the sun (symbol of growth) appears to follow a clockwise path through the sky. Below the equator the opposite is the case and there is some debate, especially in Australia and New Zealand, over whether to cast the circle and work in a clockwise direction as the rest of the world's witches do, or to work with the sun's southern direction.

Directing energy into an object to charge it is less dramatic and can be done alone or by a couple or group of people. You can visualise the energy as a stream of light, or you can let it "suggest" to you how it should look or feel. You can use a wand or athame and direct the flow of energy toward the object, or you can cup the object in your hands and draw power from around you and then project it through your fingers. As with the cone or sphere, this stream can be charged with your magical goals.

There are various other methods of magic; among them writing what you want on a piece of paper, putting it in a box, then burning or burying it, or writing runes or sigils, which you gradually reduce down into simple shapes. Robin once devised a spectacular banishing ritual where we all wrote the things we wanted to get rid of on cigarette papers, then wrapped them round tiny pinches of gunpowder (made from an authentic sixteenth-century recipe), lit them, and threw them in a cauldron where they exploded loudly. This probably comes under the "don't try this at home" category and the smell of sulphur afterward was overpowering, but the ritual was extremely satisfying, great fun, and it brought swift and positive results.

Above all, magic should be creative, intuitive, and flexible. You can try spells other people have written, but ultimately, your own spells will be best because they have been created for your specific circumstances and needs. And magic works best when it is kept simple. The basics are: raise energy; form and visualise what you want in your mind; transfer power to the candle, cord, or mental image; then let it go. Candle spells need to be recharged every day because they rely on the force of fire and because the candle needs to be completely consumed. Other spells can be left alone to do their work.

A satisfyingly large number of spells do work, bringing the desired result or something very close to it. Sometimes the spell needs to be repeated at a later date to improve conditions or help it manifest fully. All magic will work in some way, even if it isn't exactly how you planned, though some results are rapid and some arrive just when you had given up hope. However, occasionally conditions aren't right or something within you is blocking the working and it all backfires, bringing you something totally inappropriate (though not harmful), or even no visible result at all. In this situation, you must either work out what is limiting the energy, or you must accept that this idea is not going to come into being and abandon it. Be ethical, be inventive, respect others' rights and free will. Be determined, but also be prepared to accept that the way the spell works out will be best for you, even if the outcome isn't what you had dreamed it would be.

CHAPTER FIFTEEN

Autumn Equinox

Although we still enjoy mellow, sunny days, they are interspersed with spells of rain and wind, and the nights are cold. The leaves of the apple trees are turning lime green and yellow and are beginning to litter the lawn. Keeping the windblown leaves out of the pond is a nuisance, but we are afraid to use netting in case the frogs get trapped. The apples are fully ripened and so abundant that we ignore the windfalls, letting them rot back into the soil, and pick only the largest and best to make pies and cakes and crumbles. On the rowan tree the berries burn crimson, though its leaves are only just becoming tipped with orange.

Across the neighbouring gardens the autumn flowers provide a patchwork of rich colour: purple and umber, yellow, white, and bronze; After weeks of blooming the roses are spent, and there *are only a few flower heads left where a month ago geraniums blazed scarlet. On the shaggy heads of the last late sunflowers, the brown centres are turning to seed.*

From time to time our neighbour leaves produce from her garden in our porch: runner beans, fat striped marrows, gooseberries, and plums. I welcome them; my appetite always increases at this time of year and I long for soups and stews and pastry, part of the instinctive urge to put on fat before the coming of the cold, I suppose.

Down by the river, the trees are beginning to flame with colour and the wind tears the leaves from the birches by the monastery, scattering them over the grass like a far-flung handful of coins. In the early mornings, the hedges glitter with diamonds of dew caught in the gossamer nets of spiders' webs. Children pick blackberries and collect rose hips and hawthorn berries and shiny, burnished conkers. Great flocks of starlings gather in the branches and take to the sky to wheel in black formation. Geese fly over, calling to us mournfully of winter.

As the Equinox draws near, almost everyone I know seems to be having trouble adjusting to the change in rhythm, the preparation for the downward turn as all our energies become more inward flowing. My psychic faculties begin to respond to this inward current and I am more acutely sensitive than I have been during the summer months. My dream life increases, and during the day I sometimes catch movements out of the corner of my eye that reveal nothing when I turn around. One night I briefly see a white cat weaving in and out of the banisters on the landing. The last time I saw him was when our Siamese cats were small and he seemed to want to play with them. I often wondered if one of the litter had died in the womb and wanted to be near his siblings.

On the morning of the Equinox, I stand in the garden and put my hand on the trunk of the largest apple tree. It feels sleepy, the stream of inner green-gold energy slowing. The feel of the

Otherworld is all around me, almost glamorous yet very real in its own right. A blackbird settles on the fence, cocking his head to show me his yellow beak. By my head a flurry of wings announces the arrival of the robin who has been following me up and down the garden all summer. I'm afraid I must have been a disappointment to him, for I am a reluctant gardener and few worms have been turned up for him to enjoy. I bend to take up an apple and he alights to explore the exposed ground underneath, evidently finding something that satisfies him, for he is still busily pecking as I go back inside.

At dusk, Claire arrives. She is my young student and has come to do an Equinox ritual with me. I have given her a basic outline and have asked her to create something to add, and I'm very eager to see what she has come up with. She is imaginative, extremely psychic, and a powerhouse of energy. I think I must be learning almost as much from her as she is from me.

We sit and chat for a while and Claire tells me how she is progressing with some of the exercises I have given her; I'm pleased to see that she is adapting and adding to suit her own way of working. Her maturity and creativity are refreshing.

When we have centred ourselves, we begin to weave together the ritual we have both planned. I let Claire cast the circle and call the quarters; she has recently made her own wand, a beautiful creation of half-stripped willow, the places where she has removed twigs showing like dark eyes. The barrier she creates with it glows warm on my back . . . she has such personal vitality that the circle seems almost solid.

Claire has just bought a bodhran and wants to dedicate it tonight, so I suggest we do that first and that she then use it to raise power for our working. I have suggested that she write her own dedication, but she is keen to use my wording, written at the beginning of my own drumming career. She passes the drum through each of the elements in turn, saying, "I consecrate you with air—may I learn and understand how to play you. I consecrate you with fire—may I play you with creativity and energy. I consecrate you with water—may I play you with intuition and sensitivity. I consecrate you with earth—may I play you with rhythm and stability."

Clasping the drum to her, eyes closed, she then uses the invocation I had given her, "Drum, be my friend. Sing for me. Connect to the beat of my heart, and may I connect to your heartbeat. May my hands find the rhythm of your voice. Lady Brighid, guide my hands and my mind. May I learn the craft of drumming surely and with inspiration. Help my skill and enthusiasm to grow and my commitment to remain steady. Brighid, I dedicate this bodhran to you."

What Claire lacks in drumming skill she makes up for in enthusiasm and sheer driving force as she begins to play. Any qualms I had about her using a dedication appealing to Brighid, whose time is Imbolc, disappear in the face of the sheer effervescence bubbling through the circle. I ruefully acknowledge my own need to be less rigid about doing everything at the proper time. It is intention that brings results, the spirit not the letter of the law, and at this time of equilibrium I am being shown where balance is lacking in my own life.

On the altar are apples and autumn flowers, and a black and a white candle. We light the white candle for the light half of the year which is about to give way to the dark, for this is a time of balance when, as with the Spring Equinox, night and day are equal. Then we light the black candle from it to honour the dark half of the year which takes the warmth of summer away.

We can't dance round because of the restrictions of my living space, so instead we gyrate on the spot, spinning counterclockwise to banish the things we want to get rid of, naming them out loud, then spin clockwise to affirm all that we intend to work on during the winter months, all the emotional and psychological *issues that are easier to tackle once summer is over and everything withdraws.*

When we sit down afterward to meditate, we are surrounded by a sea of flame that we don't shape or send but just allow to burn. The pull of the seasonal tides is strong, yet there is balance and harmony too, for the sun has entered Libra. In my mind's eye I see a figure holding the scales; Claire says she sees Maat, the Egyptian goddess of justice.

We snuff the white candle, which will be relit at Oestara, but the black one is left to burn out to fuel our winter progress—we will carry its light on our inward journeys.

The Autumn Equinox is a solar festival that is celebrated on or around September 22, which is when the sun enters Libra, the astrological sign of balance. It should be celebrated at dawn or dusk, as these are times balanced between one state and another.

As with Oestara, day and night are equal, but the dark will soon gain power. We hang poised between outward creativity and the inward spiritual and psychological quest, though soon we will begin the descent to our own centres. For now we can pause and adjust to the change of pace.

This is the time of the second harvest, when our ancestors would have laid in stores to tide them over the scarcity and hardship of winter. For ourselves, it is time to give thanks for all we have harvested this year in our personal and spiritual lives, and time to try to balance the two. We should also acknowledge the completion of the physical harvest without which our lives would be harsh. We should do this now, even though these days the crops are often sown and reaped early, for to pay homage to the ancient cycle is to align ourselves with the natural flow of things.

Now the God has gone to the Otherworld to become the Guardian of the Gates of Death at Samhain. The Goddess, in her dual roles of Earth Mother and Hag, receives the fallen seed to rest within her during the winter months, which she will ready for spring germination. She is the tomb/womb in whose darkness we find our own rest from the individualistic, outward activity of the light half of the year.

The altar for Autumn Equinox rituals can be decorated with blackberries, apples, autumn leaves, and grain. Bring in chrysanthemums and echo their colours with dark pink, mauve, orange, and russet candles.

CHAPTER SIXTEEN

The Quarter Moons

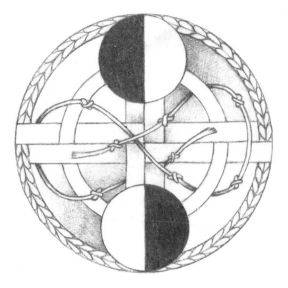

At the quarter moons, half the moon is in darkness and half is lit. These are times of balance; stopping points when the work of increase (on the waxing moon) and decrease (on the waning moon) can be assessed and then given an extra boost if necessary. These are extremely powerful lunar stations because conditions are balanced between one state and another, as are dawn and dusk, sea and shore, meadow and forest, and the two equinoxes, and such states of being are extremely mystical and potent.

Even if no magical work is done now, it is a good idea to acknowledge the quarter moons and turn their energy to inner realignment.

The first quarter falls between the new and full moons. If you are doing magical work that spans from new to full moon, then now is the time to pause and examine how things are going. Light a candle in front of your shrine, cast a circle, and meditate on the work you are doing; tune in to how things are feeling, then concentrate some extra energy on the outcome you are seeking. This time is almost like the pause on the edge of a leap—the moment when you draw breath and gather yourself as the momentum builds and you ready yourself to go forward. Spells can be reinforced at this time if you feel they need an extra charge of energy.

This is also a time to honour the balance in your relationship with others, and to ask for harmony in any partnerships that you feel are in need of more loving understanding. But remember that the balance has to be found within yourself before it can affect your relationships; you are working on your own inner needs rather than imposing on someone else.

The last quarter falls between the full and waning moons. If you are doing banishing work or any healing that involves diminishing a physical condition, then concentrate on letting go, on relinquishing the condition you need to be rid of. As with the first quarter, you can reinforce spells at this time. You can also focus on relationships, letting go of anything within yourself that is blocking love and harmony between you and another person.

Each quarter moon falls on the midpoint between the last phase and the next, and so they draw on the energies of both phases, creating a brief time of equilibrium when differences are reconciled. They are peaceful times, and yet they hold the promise of what is to come. Opening yourself to them will make you feel calm but expectant. Think of the phase you have left and what that meant to you during the current lunar cycle, then think forward with anticipation to the phase you will soon be reaching and how you can use its power.

Burn a black candle and a white candle together at the quarter moons to honour both the dark and light within yourself and all of life.

Not much has been written about the moon's quarters, and many people don't bother with them, but I feel that they are worth exploring in ritual and meditation. Pay attention to them and see whether they have significance for you personally.

CHAPTER SEVENTEEN

Waning / Dark Moon

I have watched the slender sickle morning after morning in the crystalline winter sky, its paper thin edge dissolving a little more each day until now it is gone. The moon is dark. I have been waiting for this moment. Some unknown matter is bothering me, something bubbling up from my subconscious, not yet showing its face to me—though I know it is mine and am willing to own it. Intuition tells me that I need to confront and eliminate an unresolved issue before I can move forward on my spiritual path.

So now, when the light has gone from the evening sky, I stand in my dim circle, opening to the darkness, calling on the Lady of the dark moon, on Hecate, on the Crone, she who stands at the crossroads and counsels us that we must leave the old before we can take up the new.

I feel her presence all around me, quiet and diffuse, yet deep and stern. I am drawn downward, and lower my body to a cross-legged posture in response to the weightiness I experience as my whole energy is pulled into my root chakra. As my eyes close, my inner vision comes alive and I see the curve of a black cauldron filled with leaves and loam. I am somehow in the cauldron as well as outside looking at it, and it is the earth itself, the womb of the earth, yet also my womb and the centre of my consciousness. My heart flares with a surge of love, which steadies to a quiet reassurance so that I know I am not alone and I will cope with whatever memory must be expunged.

It is quiet, so dark, like the void before the outgoing act of creation, the pause before the indrawn breath that brings prana flooding back into the body and starts the whole dance of life again (for we are reborn and recreated with each breath we take). I see bodies of plants and animals rotting and dissolving as if in a film that is being fast-forwarded. This is the place where the discarded and outworn becomes the compost that nourishes the new.

I see a spiral and then am at its centre, at the point of absolute stillness, absolute darkness; everything contained here ready to start the new cycle of manifestation, ready to begin the journey into light again. I can smell an earthy, rotting odour. It is so quiet and still that I want to stay in this state of suspended animation. Everything is at a standstill, the life currents at their lowest ebb. The Goddess does not come forth in this state—she just is. And she is everywhere.

After a long and still time I find my voice and say, "O Hecate, give me the strength to open my hands and let fall the negativity that is holding me back."

In the pit of my uterus I feel a loosening where I had not realised there was constraint. I clench my gut in momentary fear, but there is no way I can halt the emotional dissolving that has begun. Into my awareness comes a pain from long ago . . . so long, twenty years or more . . . something I had forgotten, pushed under, thought I had resolved long ago. I am powerless to prevent the flooding into consciousness of all that festering pain and hurt and despair which, uprushing, throws me back to the time I don't want to recall. But at its peak it releases me into emptiness. I am hollow but at peace.

Relief washes through me, and I reach in the dark for the bowl of earth and the black candle that I have put near to hand. Holding the candle, I draw up the threads of negativity that I have disgorged and focus them into the dark wax. When I am done, I light the candle and push it into the bowl of earth. As it burns down it will infuse the earth with the residue of my suffering, will transmute it. This will become compost in which I will plant flower seeds (symbolic of fresh goals) when the new moon comes. Nature always fills a vacuum: that which I have relinquished must be replaced with something to flourish during a fresh cycle.

I am cleansed and healing can now take place, the healing followed by growth.

The moon is said to be waning from about two to three days after full till just before the new moon occurs. At the end of this period the moon is no longer visible. The waning moon is ruled by the Wisewoman or Grandmother and the dark moon by the Crone, though these two phases can be treated as one. During this entire period, the life force gradually subsides till, just before the new moon is due, everything is flat and subdued and people complain of tiredness or apathy.

Magically, this is the wrong time to begin anything new, and in fact this is the best time of all for banishing anything unwanted, including ill health or disease, and eliminating that which is no longer of use. You can begin the process of elimination slowly, starting just after the full moon phase and working day by day till the dark moon. Or you can do

one powerful ritual at the dark moon itself. Some examples
would be losing excess weight, banishing lack from your life,
dissolving blocks. Always remember to have something in
mind that can grow in the place of that which you have discarded; for example, if you are eliminating fat, replace it
with a healthily balanced body; if you are banishing lack,
replace it with plenty of whatever you are needing. State
this intention after the banishing ritual. Also, always
remember to work with the proviso that you harm no one,
yourself included (a friend of mine worked for rapid weight
loss, but didn't specify that it happen without damaging herself, and subsequently spent three days with violent sickness
and diarrhea!), and that nobody's free will is transgressed—
you don't have the right to buy prosperity at somebody else's
expense, for instance.

Burn a black candle for banishing. Rites at this time can
be conducted in an unlit circle, or with only one dark central candle burning. The incense you use should have a sombre tone, such as myrrh or patchouli. Rituals may also be
centred around spiritual searching or meditation, and this is
the optimum time for an inward journey.

CHAPTER EIGHTEEN

Samhain

Although the days are sometimes overcast, the nights are clear and starry and the ground grows hard with frost. The brave colours of early October are gone and only a few crackling brown leaves now cling stubbornly to the oak, the last of the trees to lose his clothing. The hedgehogs have curled up somewhere to hibernate and, but for central heating, most of us would probably want to follow suit. When the wind blows it is fierce and bitter, but there are still days when the sun gives a false intimation of warmth and the sky is a flawless but brittle blue.

Everywhere I shop I see pumpkins—in the Covered Market, on the Wednesday market, and even in the supermarkets. They are every shade of orange and in fat or elongated ellipses of every size, from a small football to monsters that would fill your arms.

There are turnips, too, and candles and witches' masks, cats, ghosts, and all the other paraphernalia of Halloween. Small people with scary faces and outstretched hands knock on the door demanding "Trick or treat" for at least a week before the event. I grow tired of handing out coins and telling them not to frighten old ladies; but by the end of October they are wanting "Penny for the Guy" (a British tradition similar to trick-or-treat) instead and the nights are vivid with premature fireworks.

The commercialism passes me by, for I am lost in the intensity and beauty of the original festival of Samhain from which both Halloween and Bonfire Night derive. This is the Feast of the Dead, the time when the God becomes the Lord of the Gates of Death and when those who have died and those as yet unborn can draw close to us. The Wheel of the Year turns down into the roots of winter, the light and life of summer are spent . . . and yet nothing is lost to us forever, and already the first faint bulges show where twig and branch will erupt into new leaf at spring.

On October 31 we work hard all day scooping out pumpkins and making soup and pies with the strange fibrous flesh. Some of us make turnip lanterns too, as our ancestors would have done. When all is ready, when the log fire is blazing and candles light the squashy orange faces with their jagged teeth and geometric eyes, when the children have eagerly donned their costumes and emerge as witches, devils, and black cats, we fill the cauldron with water and float apples inside, then bring food to the table and prepare to honour our dead.

Everybody has lost someone they love in the last year. We write their names on slips of paper, prop up photos, compose poems. Small furry creatures, a puppy, a mouse, a guinea pig, and two rats are greeted, along with somebody's aunt and someone else's childhood friend who died, shockingly, only a month ago. All are equally loved and equally mourned. Each is honoured with a lit Hanukkah candle pushed into damp earth. Quips are made about the fire brigade as the candles blaze!

In the dancing light the air shimmers and grows thin. Even the most prosaic of us falls silent as the room fills up with the presence of the unseen who have come to share our spread. This is the time that is no time, when the gateway between the worlds stands wide and we wait on the threshold of the Celtic new year.

As we eat, we take it in turns to recite a poem, drum, read a short tale. The children act out fairy stories or pronounce wicked spells that make us shudder in mock horror and then roar with laughter, and the solemn atmosphere dissolves into gaiety and the contentment of shared warmth and friendship.

When the others have left, our group of four stay talking round the table, drowsy with food and the warmth of the fire. I stare into the water-filled cauldron and idly let images drift to the surface of my mind, but they are scenes from long ago, when everyone in a settlement would have gathered round the huge fire between their dwellings to eat and drink and indulge in riotous entertainment. I see tall men and women dressed in brown homespun garments, strange designs tattooed in blue along their arms and cheekbones; I see children running wildly, laughing—this is the time between times when mischief is abroad. The heat from the fire reaches out and many of the people have thrown off their overgarments despite the winter chill.

I shake my head to clear the pictures. The Trickster is abroad tonight and I have no way of telling if my vision is true, only a product of my mind, or a conglomeration of all the Celtic source material I have seen. Then Nick fetches a tarot deck and reads for us till it is time to prepare the room upstairs for our Samhain rite.

When all is ready, Julia, a friend from London, arrives to join us. She is a solitary witch but sometimes likes to celebrate with others, especially at the festivals. She brings a huge bunch of chrysanthemums and they sit on our altar spreading their sharp fragrance through the room—the flowers of death, purple, cream, and bronze. We have worked with Julia before and can easily accommodate her energy, though the balance of the group shifts from a stable four to a more dynamic five, and the space rapidly fills with vitality, though the powers we invoke remain sombre and deep.

Our drumming is slow and steady and takes us into ourselves as we sit cross-legged near the altar. I glance at the others: Robin's face is alert, as though he is listening for something; Moira's is tranquil; Julia's black hair has swung forward and masks her expression, but her whole body is relaxed and I feel her awareness slipping away and onto another level.

Then the room grows hazy; I feel remote and calm, and a faint whisper of movement displaces the air around me, then is still. I feel my father's presence and see his face behind my closed eyelids, not as it was at the end of his life but as I remember it from when I was a child. He has been dead for many years. We were unable to be close while he was alive, unable to bridge our differences or transcend the startlingly opposed values of our generations. But from time to time I sense him near me, as now, and know that we are building a better relationship across our two different levels of being. Love surrounds me briefly—I sense his awkwardness and my own at the open sharing of emotion— then he is gone.

Afterward, we replenish the dark-smelling incense and then pass round the witches' mirror. Robin says he sees people sitting in a graveyard feasting, Nick sees the God standing in blackness but surrounded by the souls of a myriad of animals, human included. I see only the cold earth, rotting leaves, and a vast empty place where there are no stars. Melancholy wreathes up out of the winter ground. Death is inevitable, implacable, and yet it is only one side of a duality, the other part of which is life. Everything has its allotted timespan and then transforms to another state or level of being. Everything regenerates and returns; even we come back *again and again to meet with our companions of before and experience another round of the dance.*

When we bless and pass round our spiced chalice and apple cake, we wish each other Happy New Year; for though the Wheel of the Year commences its round at Yule with the sun's rebirth, to our Celtic ancestors the New Year was now.

Samhain (pronounced *Sowain*, to rhyme with cow) is a cross-quarter fire festival and lasts from October 31 to November 2. It is sacred to the Cailleagh and to the God as Keeper of the Underworld. These days, we celebrate after dark on October 30, but in Celtic times the celebrations would have gone on for at least two weeks. All Souls, the later Christian-isation, falls on November 2. Many other cultures also have some sort of festival for the dead around now, and this is apt, for it is the time presided over by the astrological sign of Scorpio, which rules death and regeneration.

This is the Celtic New Year, another "time that is no time," poised between the old year and the new. Someone once pointed out to me that, though the buds become fatter in spring, they are already forming now. This is also the Feast of the Dead, when people of old put out food for the ancestors and invited them to return on this night, when the door between the worlds stands open.

The festival is symbolic of death and rebirth, the death of summer but the promise that spring will emerge from the dark womb of the Earth Mother. The Goddess comes as the Crone, the Cailleagh, the deathly bringer of winter cold and ice in whose belly the life forces sleep. Yet she is pregnant with the Sun God, who will be born at Yule. Her mate, the old God, stands guarding the gates of death and birth, awaiting his own renaissance.

In ancient times, when winter grazing was scarce and only breeding stock could be kept, most other stock was slaughtered, their meat salted down for consumption during the cold months. So there was a surfeit of food at this festival, enough for a community to eat as much as they wanted and still have plenty to share with the dead—the last time they would be able to fully satisfy their hunger before Yule.

Now is the point in the year's cycle when we too can honour our dead, especially those who have gone over in the last year, and when they can traverse the route between the different "levels" of being to be with us. Photos of them can be displayed, their names can be written on paper, and a candle can be burned for each of them. Because the veil between the worlds is very thin now, this is a traditional time for scrying, crystal gazing, and other forms of divination. Girls in former ages would look over their shoulder into a mirror at Halloween and hope to see their future husband's face, or they would peel an apple and let its skin fall to form the initial of his name.

In our lives, we have to complete the inward turning and die to a phase of outer activity, in keeping with the short days and long nights of winter. We need to become more introspective, go deeper within ourselves, and confront the inner reaches of our psyches and all that that may hold for us. Yet at the same time we grow closer to each other as we live a more home-orientated existence than in summer.

The trimmings for this festival are chrysanthemums, the flowers of death; apples, the Celtic fruit of the dead; and pumpkin and turnip lanterns cut into skull-like faces, their eyes, noses, and mouths lit by candles.

Samhain teaches us that on a deep level there is no death, but only change and the growth that it brings.

CHAPTER NINETEEN

Initiation

Whether or not to become initiated is a choice that sooner or later presents itself to many witches. There are various reasons for this. Some people feel that they cannot be proper witches without undergoing some sort of validating ceremony. Others feel an inner need that is so strong they are driven to assuage it. Still others love the prospect of being on a high for a while, of feeling special, of enjoying a celebration of which they are the focus. For some it is their only access to the covens or traditions that require initiation before they will admit new members. Then there are those who have no desire for initiation at all and are perfectly happy to continue their practice as they have always done. The whole issue is deeply personal and cannot be decided by anyone but oneself. This is in contrast to the majority of religions, where a child is raised within a certain creed and is inducted fully into it when the appropriate age is reached.

Initiation is a serious business! Once undergone it cannot be reversed, and whatever the original motives of the partic-ipator, it will bring changes into their life. Having said that, initiation is also an inward matter—the outward ceremony may trigger responses or set the scene, but the real initiation takes place deep within the psyche. Outer initiation often also reflects an inner change that has already taken place. All of us are undergoing initiations as we pass from one phase to another or navigate the major rites of passage such as the first sexual experience, marriage, or the death of someone close. Initiation itself is a form of death and rebirth. In many native cultures, for instance, adolescents undergo a symbolic death to mark the passing of their old life as they enter puberty. Those of us who have chosen to work consciously with our own spirituality will inevitably experience major gateways or turning points periodically, when things appear to open up and life experiences inten-sify. Of course, this applies to everyone to some degree, but self-development accelerates and deepens the process.

My own initiations took the form of four rites, separated by many years. The first was a self-initiation, a profound experience that turned around the entire way I looked at life and set me firmly on my current path; it was an acknowledg-ment that I am and have always been a witch, and of my voluntary commitment to being a Priestess of the Goddess and the God. The second rite was a formal initiation into a coven that was within one of the "officially" accepted Wic-can traditions. This outer recognition of an inner state that had already occurred was less profound, though still very meaningful, and served to balance up certain aspects of my personality that I had trouble reconciling alone; further initiations have served to deepen my commitment to my chosen path.

Let me make it quite clear that initiation does not make you a better or more important witch. There is currently a regrettable tendency among some people to think that only "properly" initiated witches are authentic. But some leading authorities within the Craft today have either never been initiated, have done a self-initiation, or have started their own initiatory tradition. This does not detract from the value of what they have to teach. Many of us have undergone initiation in previous lives, and the stamp of this is upon us still, whether or not we renew it in this lifetime. It is the inner spiritual opening that makes an initiation valid rather than the "correctness" of the body bestowing it. In our modern preoccupation with educational and business status and qualifications, we tend to apply the same criteria to our spiritual lives, and this is wrong.

Furthermore, it is not necessary for all members of a group or coven to have been initiated in order to work together productively. Within the coven to which I belong, two of us have been initiated and two have not. I don't consider any of us to be wiser or more genuine than the others. We all contribute equally to our rituals, all balance each other, all have equally valid and original contributions to make. And while I have had the "genuine" article, my fellow was given an almost identical "copy" administered by someone who had not received full initiation herself . . . yet our experiences were very similar and I do not consider mine to be more true than his.

Nor does being an initiate necessarily make you suddenly more psychic or esoterically informed. Many people are natural psychics from birth; many others who have been initiated for years and are running their own covens cheerfully admit that they aren't particularly psychically aware—they have experience and strengths in other areas, such as an ability to organise rituals, or special skills in teaching or dealing with people. Anyway, psychic and spiritual awareness can be two different things and many highly enlightened people do not use their paranormal faculties at all, seeing them as merely another ability along with art or music.

Ultimately, initiation is about being willing to confront yourself honestly, being ready for a great deal of inner growth and self-realisation, and committing yourself to serving the Goddess and the God in whatever way is appropriate for you personally. By dedicating ourselves to Goddess and God, we are serving the life force that is part of us and of which we are a part, and by so doing we are furthering the expansion and awareness of life itself.

If you desire initiation, it will become necessary for you to either seek out an individual or group who will perform this for you, or devise a ceremony of your own. Whichever route you choose to take, approach it in a serious manner; think carefully about why you want this path and what you think it will bring you. Be sensible and careful about finding contacts. It is quite difficult to find traditional Wiccan covens who will be willing to initiate you, but there are a number of power trippers of dubious intent who may be happy to latch on to you and take credit for your spiritual education. Aside from this, perfectly nice people who may sincerely want to help you may have no opening for new coven members; they are unlikely to initiate you and then turn you loose to find your own way, especially as one purpose of initiation into a group is to become a participating member. In Britain, one way of finding help is to join one of the better known pagan support organisations and go to their official meetings or local gatherings—other countries have similar organisations. Groups such as these can be located on the Internet or in the back of many pagan publications. Don't invite someone you don't know to your home or go to their home unaccompanied; meet them in a public place and take someone with you. This is common sense: most pagans are decent people, but there are some nasty impostors around too. Be careful!

The common waiting period before initiation to a coven is a year and a day. This is not necessarily because the other members think you are inexperienced, but because they need time to adjust to you, as you do to them, before you are ready to work intensively together. In practice, this time may be shorter or longer. Sadly, not all high priestesses and high priests are aware enough to judge the readiness of a candidate and so prospective coven members can sometimes be kept waiting much longer than this.

Whether you make someone else responsible for guiding your path to initiation or make your way alone, it is standard practice to undergo some form of prior training and preparation. If you already have a great deal of knowledge, and these days—with the expansion of readily available information and the "shopping around" that people do whilst determining their direction—many people do, then you need to find a way to take that knowledge to another level. If you have already learned about the elemental correspondences, for example, then find ways to experience them firsthand. Go out into the countryside and commune with the elements there; open yourself to the sky, the earth, the river, and listen to what they have to teach you. Look into astrology or tarot and see how the elements are used in those systems. There is always a way to expand our awareness further.

If you know what you want and feel *in your heart of hearts* that you are ready and that this is the path for you and are going to do a self-initiation, then give yourself a programme to work through and tasks to solve. You might plan to make a wand or learn about the runes, for instance. Take things steadily and give yourself several months in which to prepare, if necessary. If you don't rush, then you will have plenty of opportunity for reflection and the chance to change your mind. Going forward with initiation must be an absolute inner conviction. Some people will need less time, some more . . . only you can decide what is appropriate for you.

Prepare for your initiation ritual as you would any other, paying the same attention to yourself and your space. Approach the event calmly; meditate before, if possible; make sure the room is quiet and has been cleaned thoroughly. You might want to put special oil or herbs in your bath, wear a special garment (or go skyclad), put beautiful flowers on your altar, and choose a candle that you can burn afterward to light your new path. You might consider obtaining a piece of jewellery that symbolises your initiation for you and which you will wear from now on. Second degree Alexandrian witches are sometimes given a silver ring by their initiator.

It is not my place to write an initiation for you. If you are serious about it, then you should be reading and learning as much as possible in preparation, and that includes background knowledge and ideas on the rite itself. But this will be your special time and what you say and do needs to come from you, from your own heart, mind, and spirit. In previous ages, initiation rites were often terrifying, painful, or dangerous—or all three. They were designed to shock the participant into another level of awareness or to mimic death and rebirth. These days, it is no longer regarded as necessary to put people through this type of trauma, at least in our well-fed Western culture, where physical strength and survival are not requirements. Curling into a fetal position and then stretching out and lighting a candle is a simple and beautiful way to show that you are being born into a new life. Try changing from one set of clothes to another or going naked like a newborn, then donning a garment to represent the state you are coming into. Afterward, enjoy a period of quiet contemplation before partaking of the usual food and drink.

If you do not go down the path of initiation, this does not mean that you are a lesser spiritual being or that you won't grow and change. Sometimes the same realisations can accumulate over the passage of time, unfolding gradually and gently. Sometimes, too, inner commitment needs no outer declaration or ceremony. Whichever way you choose, you will walk with the gods. Blessed Be.

Glossary

Alexandrian: Contemporary branch of initiatory Wicca founded by Alex Sanders.

Astral Plane: Plane of existence interpenetrating but less dense than the material world.

Athame: The ritual knife used to direct energy and cast the circle. Usually double-edged and with a black handle. It is never used to draw blood and the only thing that should ever be cut with it is the cake at a handfasting.

Aura: Sheath of subtle energy surrounding the body.

Autumn Equinox: One of the eight seasonal festivals. Second harvest. Equal days and nights but with the nights about to increase in length. Occurs around September 21.

Beltane: One of the eight seasonal festivals. Centres on the marriage of the Flower Maiden and the Horned Lord of the Greenwood. April 30 to May 1.

Book of Shadows: A journal of spells, rituals, dreams, meditations, and so on that is kept by individual witches.

Chakras: Energy centres in the auric field. Chakra is Hindu for wheel, and these centres are said to revolve like wheels of force when activated.

Chalice: A goblet or cup used to contain wine, juice, spring water, and the like at the end of a ritual. It belongs to the element water.

Cone of power: Spiral of active power shaped by witches during magical working. Can also be sphere or pillar shaped.

Coven: A small group of witches who regularly come together to work ritual or magic and celebrate the festivals.

Etheric Energy: The psychic energy used to shape the ritual circle.

Gardnerian: Contemporary branch of initiatory Wicca; founded by Gerald Gardner.

Handfasting: A pagan marriage ceremony.

Hedgewitch: A witch who usually prefers to work alone or with a partner, often in an earthy way with an emphasis on herbalism and country lore.

Imbolc: One of the eight seasonal festivals. The festival of purification. February 1.

Karma: Law of cause and effect. Whatever you do, for good or bad, is ultimately your responsibility and the energy triggered by the act will come back to you eventually. This has to do with universal harmony and balance and has nothing to do with punishment (though it can feel like it sometimes).

Lammas: One of the eight seasonal festivals. The first harvest—grain harvest. Sacrifice of the God and John Barleycorn. August 1.

Oestara/Spring Equinox: One of the eight seasonal festivals. The time of rebirth in early spring. Equal day and night with the days about to increase in length. March 21.

Pentacle: A disk bearing a pentagram, and, possibly, other symbols. Food, materials for spells, and so on can be placed on it on the altar. It belongs to earth.

Pentagram: Five pointed star. Has been adopted as the symbol for witchcraft and paganism. The points represent the four elements and spirit.

Samhain: One of the eight seasonal festivals. Halloween. The Feast of the Dead. The Celtic New Year. Time when the veil between the worlds is thin and we can commune with the Ancestors. October 31 to November 1.

Scrying: A method of divination that uses a reflective surface such as a mirror, bowl of water, or crystal ball to defocus the mind to assist clairvoyance.

Skyclad: A Wiccan term meaning unclothed. Many (but by no means all) witches work ritual this way.

Smudging: Wafting incense or herbal smoke over people, objects, or ritual space to cleanse them. Widely used by practitioners of the Native American paths.

Solitary: A witch who works alone, either by choice or because of the difficulty of finding a coven.

Summer Solstice: One of the eight seasonal festivals. Midsummer festival of the sun's maximum power. Occurs around June 21.

The Craft: Witchcraft; sometimes called the Craft of the Wise.

Wand: A short stave of wood used to direct energy in spell crafting. Can be used instead of the athame to cast the circle. It is ruled by fire.

Wheel of the Year: The round of eight festivals and the seasonal cycle.

Wiccan: Initiatory witchcraft including Gardnerian and Alexandrian Wicca.

Yule/Winter Solstice: The sun's rebirth. One of the eight seasonal festivals. Occurs around December 21.

Living Wicca
A Further Guide for the Solitary Practitioner

SCOTT CUNNINGHAM

Living Wicca is the long-awaited sequel to Scott Cunningham's wildly successful *Wicca: a Guide for the Solitary Practitioner.* This book is for those who have made the conscious decision to bring their Wiccan spirituality into their everyday lives. It provides solitary practitioners with the tools and added insights that will enable them to blaze their own spiritual paths—to become their own high priests and priestesses.

Living Wicca takes a philosophical look at the questions, practices, and differences within Witchcraft. It covers the various tools of learning available to the practitioner, the importance of secrecy in one's practice, guidelines to performing ritual when ill, magical names, initiation, and the Mysteries. It discusses the benefits of daily prayer and meditation, making offerings to the gods, how to develop a prayerful attitude, and how to perform Wiccan rites when away from home or in emergency situations.

Unlike any other book on the subject, *Living Wicca* is a step-by-step guide to creating your own Wiccan tradition and personal vision of the gods, designing your personal ritual and symbols, developing your own book of shadows, and truly living your Craft.

0-87542-184-9
208 pp., 6 x 9, illus. $12.95

Inside a Witches' Coven
EDAIN McCOY

Inside a Witches' Coven gives you an insider's look at how a real Witches' coven operates, from initiation and secret vows to parting rituals. You'll get step-by-step guidance for joining or forming a coven, plus sage advice and exclusive insights to help you decide which group is the right one for you.

Maybe you're thinking about joining a coven, but don't know what to expect, or how to make contacts. Perhaps you already belong to a coven, but your group needs ideas for organizing a teaching circle or mediating conflicts. Either way, you're sure to find *Inside a Witches' Coven* a practical source of wisdom.

Joining a coven can be an important step in your spiritual life. Before you take that step, let a practicing Witch lead you through the hidden inner workings of a Witches' coven.

1-56718-666-1
224 pp., 5¼ x 8   **$9.95**

To order, call 1-800-THE MOON
Prices subject to change without notice

Covencraft
Witchcraft for Three or More

AMBER K

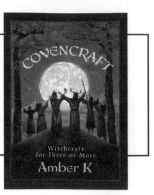

Here is the complete guidebook for anyone who desires to practice Witchcraft in a caring, challenging, well-organized spiritual support group: a coven. Whether you hope to learn more about this ancient spiritual path, are a coven member wanting more rewarding experiences in your group, are looking for a coven to join or are thinking of starting one, or are a Wiccan elder gathering proven techniques and fresh ideas . . . this book is for you.

Amber K shares what she as learned about beginning and maintaining healthy covens in her twenty years as a Wiccan priestess. Learn what a coven is, how it works, and how you can make your coven experience more effective, enjoyable, and rewarding. Plus, get practical hands-on guidance in the form of sample Articles of Incorporation, internet resources, sample by-laws, and sample budgets. Seventeen ritual scripts are also provided.

1-56718-018-3
480 pp., 7 x 10, illus. $17.95